Radioactive Documentary

Keine Zukunft

Ohne Vergangenheit

Bergbautraditionsverein   Wismut

Radioactive Documentary

Filming the Nuclear Environment after the Cold War

Helen Hughes

Bristol, UK / Chicago, USA

First published in the UK in 2021 by
Intellect, The Mill, Parnall Road, Fishponds, Bristol, BS16 3JG, UK

First published in the USA in 2021 by
Intellect, The University of Chicago Press, 1427 E. 60th Street,
Chicago, IL 60637, USA

A catalogue record for this book is available from
the British Library.

Copy editor: MPS Limited
Cover designer: Aleksandra Szumlas
Cover image: *Tamed Power*, Achim Kühn, 1985, KT steel, stainless steel sculpture,
Nuclear Research Institute Dresden-Rossendorf, Dresden, Germany. Commissioned by
the Academy of Sciences of the GDR, 5.5 metres. Photograph taken by Achim Kühn.
Frontispiece image: *No future without the past*, plaque placed by the Bergbautra-
ditionsverein, Wismut, on the Schmirchauer Höhe, in Thuringia, Germany. Photo-
graph taken by Helen Hughes.
Production managers: Faith Newcombe and Georgia Earl
Typesetter: MPS Limited

Print ISBN 978-1-78938-384-3
ePDF ISBN 978-1-78938-385-0
ePUB ISBN 978-1-78938-386-7

Printed and bound by CPI

To find out about all our publications, please visit our website.
There you can subscribe to our e-newsletter, browse or download our current
catalogue and buy any titles that are in print.

www.intellectbooks.com

This is a peer-reviewed publication.

I have studied the conductivity of air under the influence of the rays from uranium, discovered by Becquerel, and I have investigated whether other substances than the compounds of uranium were capable of making the air a conductor of electricity.
I have obtained good photographic impressions with uranium, uranous oxide, pitchblende, chalcolite, thorium oxide. These substances act at small distances, whether through air, through glass or through aluminium.

– Mme Sklodowska Curie (1898), 'Rays emitted by the compounds of uranium and thorium', translated and reproduced in Romer (1970: 65–67).

Contents

Figures

Preface

This book was prompted by the debates around the nuclear renaissance that was declared in the new millennium. It was a moment when President Barack Obama, in an attempt to get a climate change bill through the Senate, included financial support to build new nuclear power plants in the United States, the first for 30 years. It seemed like a strange new moment in which one set of problems was to be traded for another and, having written on environmental documentaries or 'eco-docs', I was interested in how the issue was reflected in documentary cinema (Hughes 2014). In the course of researching for this book the subject shifted somewhat from the role of documentary in debates about energy and the future to its role in debates about the past and the industrial legacy. The nuclear renaissance was stalled by the accident at the Fukushima Daiichi nuclear power station in 2011, a moment that accelerated the shift from new energy futures to the urgency of dealing with the legacy of the past.

There are many Cold War documentaries emerging through the process of digitization, which have been important for this project, but I decided to stick nevertheless to the post–Cold War study that I planned. My interest is in this moment as one of change for which the form of the documentary provides some evidence. Documentary as a form poses questions about the expression of opinion. If there is a shift in public perceptions of nuclear power because of climate change, how does it show up? Can documentary make it show up, or bring it about? Is there a moment between, a discernible before and after? And if the triple disaster in Fukushima changed minds again, why was the renaissance so fragile? Perhaps nothing changed at all in fact besides the debate itself.

One documentary film from before the end of the Cold War has emerged as an artefact that does capture a moment of change. *Chernobyl. Khronika trudnykh nedel* (*Chernobyl: A Chronicle of Difficult Weeks*, 1987) was made by the Soviet filmmaker Vladimir Shevchenko using footage recorded by him and his film crew following the nuclear accident at Chernobyl in April 1986. This film is by now reasonably well known. There is also a second film, *Kolokol Chernobyl* (*The Toxin of Chernobyl*) (Sergienko 1987), which was made from footage shot from 28 May to 26 June in early September 1986 and credited to a collective by the Central Documentary Film Studios in Moscow. It found its way into the collection of Stanley Forman, a distributor of films donated by socialist countries during the

Cold War, which are now held at the British Film Institute archive where I viewed it. Both of these films document the aftermath of the accident which is widely understood not only to have contributed to the end of the Union of Soviet Socialist Republics (USSR or hereafter the Soviet Union) but also to have changed global awareness of nuclear issues.

These two films are significant to this book for different reasons. The rather tricky title *Radioactive Documentary* is partly inspired by the reception of *Chernobyl: A Chronicle of Difficult Weeks* through the work of the British artists Jane and Louise Wilson, particularly their *Toxic Camera*, as well as through the work of the London-based critic and artist Susan Schuppli. In the course of the film, Shevchenko refers to the 'voice' of radioactivity, an idea that is striking for the way in which it asserts the directness of the audiovisual experience and circumvents the idea of radioactivity as invisible. The scene is shot from one of the helicopters Shevchenko joined to fly over and film reactor 4 as it was throwing out a continuous thick plume of radioactive ash. In the film Shevchenko accompanies the shots with a voice-over commentary that explains that he had interpreted some white flashing on the film as faults in the original stock. 'We thought this film was defective', reads the subtitle 'But we were mistaken. This is how radiation looks'. When the film is running the blemishes are experienced as flashing lights that are almost sensed rather than seen as they pass so quickly.

In a film theoretical analysis the artist and cultural theorist Schuppli (2010) identifies Shevchenko's film with those which contain moments when the material environment and the social world of documentary become intimately linked, triggering a strong affective response, a feeling of dread, in the viewer. She refers to it as like a radioactive fossil, suggesting how an account of the physical quality of the exposed film stock – a kind of literal analysis of it – and an understanding of the images as pictorial representations of a place and time, can be combined. It is an idea that I have translated into the title, radioactive documentary. Significant about Schuppli's account for the development of this book is its recognition of the exposure of film stock to ionizing radiation as cognate with its exposure to light or electromagnetic waves in general. This creates an indexical mark out of the scene that links it with the long running discussion in film studies about documentary realism. The marks on Shevchenko's film bring out a particular issue for documentary filmmaking in the representation of radioactivity. It is often said that it cannot be seen, felt or heard so that other ways have to be found to make it visible. Schuppli has drawn attention to the ways in which this kind of visibility connects viewers with institutions and their forensic apparatus.

In the films referred to in this book two units of measurement for radioactivity are also referred to in sequences designed to make radioactivity more visible – a legacy unit called the röntgen and the contemporary unit called the sievert. The use of these units in the films is not always helpful and it is clear that their use is part of an evolving process in public communication about radioactivity itself. The units can be understood as different ways of answering the question sometimes posed in the films: what is radioactivity? The United States Nuclear Regulatory Commission describes four different objects of measurement on its website: radioactivity, exposure, absorbed dose, and equivalent dose. For film representations these different units actually pose the question in a different way – which is not always noted by reporters. How radioactive is this object? How radioactive is the environment around me? How much radiation has entered the body of the person on-screen? How dangerous is the dose of radiation I would receive in the situation seen on-screen? The röntgen, one of the units referred to, relates to the question of exposure – how radioactive is that environment – and the sievert answers to the question of equivalent dose – what would the danger be for me? These questions show how the perspective in radioactivity measurements shifts from the object to the environment and to the exposure of the human body, a change in perspective that characterizes environmental issues more generally, and poses the challenge and the opportunity for documentary representations of radioactivity.

Shevchenko referred to the audiovisual combination of blotches on his film with the crescendo on the Geiger counter as the 'voice of radiation'. Similar blotches appear in the film made by the Central Documentary Film Studios in Moscow, *The Toxin of Chernobyl* which has been understood as propaganda with its opening quotation from Gorbachev: 'The accident at Chernobyl shows again what an abyss will open if nuclear war befalls mankind for inherent in the nuclear stockpile are thousands upon thousands of disasters far more horrible than the Chernobyl one'. This film integrates its account of the emergency response into a portrait of the suffering of people being evacuated, being measured for their exposure and talking about those who have fallen ill and died. The flashes appear on a sequence about the clearing of the roofs above the stricken reactor and in the long grasses of the countryside around the reactor, but rather than reading 'this is what radiation looks like' the commentary reads 'the flashes were given various explanations by the physicists'. The discursive understanding of how the film stock interacts with radiation is here left open to alternative interpretations creating differing relationships with the image and hence also with feeling. Instead of focusing on radioactivity, the film channels emotions into anger about the people who caused the accident through 'acceleration' who 'should be shot'.

Taking the example of *Chernobyl Toxin*, this study follows the openness of 'various explanations' allowing for different readings of the physical effects of radiation. Thinking about it in terms of the film stock, the flashes could be directly caused by gamma rays or by high-frequency photons released by them or there might have been contamination in the camera in the form of radioactive dust particles that could have later damaged the film. Switching from the physical to the social register, on the other hand, if a kind of Copernican turn is enacted, and the flashes are seen not as accidental effects or a world gone wrong, but as the organizing principle in the image, a different representational reading can also emerge.

The photographic plate that revealed uranium salts to be a source of light in Henri Becquerel's drawer is generally restricted in its meaning to the discovery of radioactivity, but the direction of agency can be reversed. It is also an image of the first step in a reorganization of the human world around new knowledge. The interaction between the camera at Chernobyl and the physical world produces images that show how the human world is organized in response to the presence of radioactivity. Were the camera to have been there a few days earlier it would have produced images of people working at a nuclear power station, organized in shifts to tend to the instrumentation monitoring the performance of the reactor. After the accident the camera produces images of a different workforce, the scientists, soldiers and medical staff called in to contain the accident and tend to the local population.

One of the arguments that has emerged in writing *Radioactive Documentary* is that cinema pictures the ways in which radioactivity has reorganized the social world. In *The Toxin of Chernobyl* the focus is on the effects of the scattering of radionuclides carried by the wind to villages and farming land north of the power station. Before the accident the land was organized around the production of agricultural produce. The people lived in villages spread out across the region and were organized collectively. The camera cannot register the radionuclides without distorting the picture but protected from the dust it can show how the social world is reorganized around their presence such as the apples left lying on the ground, the abandoned villages, the people waiting uncertainly on the periphery of the zone and the medical stations where people wait to be monitored.

In *The Toxin of Chernobyl* the villagers come to the camera knowing that it will place their testimony in the chronology of images of the disaster. The persistent presence of the cameras around the accident eventually begins to change from interaction with the physical reality of the accident into an intervention in which the people begin to try to direct the debate about its causes and effects. This interplay between interaction and intervention is important as it brings in the all-important question about the future of the industry. *The Toxin of Chernobyl* ends with several statements such as 'Our country needs lots of energy' and 'we cannot go back to the Stone Age' and the striking ending states: 'They tried to subordinate the greatest discovery of our age, the energy of the atom, to departmental interests. We are on the threshold of a new age, a new millennium. Mankind must learn to think and live differently'.

In the course of researching for this book it became clear from these two films that a change in perspective that can be noted in the films after the Cold War was already underway in the films being made in the immediate aftermath of Chernobyl. All of these responses point to the documentary camera as reflexive, showing the physical and social reality of the new nuclear landscape. The title *Radioactive Documentary* is thus not only about the 'voice' of radioactivity but also about the more explicit process of understanding the camera as immersed in the industrial modernity of the post-war period, with a role to play, in the terms of Ulrich Beck's analysis of the risk society, in the new kind of 'reflexive modernity' that emerged from the risks that industry has produced (1992).

As will be discussed in the introduction the imbricated camera is one that has provoked much discussion in the field of documentary studies. A sculptural work by the artists Jane and Louise Wilson referring to Shevchenko's camera adds radioactivity to the idea of the reflexive camera in a productive way. Solidly mounted on concrete and cast in bronze, *Toxic Camera: Konvas Avtomat* appears at first to stand in a metonymic relationship with the soviet director who recorded the heroes as they responded to the accident at Chernobyl. His death turns the sculpture into a memorial highlighting the documentary commitment to record and make public what happened. The *New York Times* reported Shevchenko's death with a quotation from an introduction to the premiere of his film at the Soviet film festival in Tbilisi, which praised him as 'an outstanding man who gave his life so that we and our descendants could see with our own eyes all the horror and depth of the Chernobyl tragedy' (Reuters 1987).

As such the sculpture in its solidity invites some thought on documentary as a social process that brings out the tragedy in Shevchenko's relationship with his camera. In a review of the film as it was distributed in 1991 as part of a DVD set entitled *The Glasnost Film Festival* James Krukones wrote, 'Shevchenko's film is especially provocative for criticizing the incompetence that allowed the accident to occur in the first place and then worsen in the absence of an immediate response' (Krukones 1991: 1137). This understands *Chernobyl: A Chronicle of Difficult Weeks* as the product of Soviet President Mikhail Gorbachev's reformist policy of transparency and openness or *glasnost*. The film is concerned primarily with giving an account of the Soviet response to the catastrophe and due to the permission to film anywhere on the site, and the filmmaker's willingness to do so, it is a truly remarkable example of the observational style of documentary filmmaking. As Krukones points out, the film is a tribute from start to finish to the hundreds of individuals involved in the response who managed 'to discover in themselves something they had never expected'.

All of these points about the heroism of the documentary filmmaker lead to a final point in this preface to the study regarding the relationship between the body of the camera and the body of the camera operator. In the narrative of the disaster and its aftermath, the film might be said to be complicit with the way in which the accident brought out a tendency in Soviet society towards self-sacrifice which Shevchenko, in his disregard for the dangers to his own health, also displayed. The bronze sculpture thus represents a heroism that by 2012 – the date of the sculpture – had become entangled in the spirit of doubt about the meaning of such sacrifice.

Svetlana Alexievich's *Chernobyl Prayer,* a collection of reflections by Belorussian witnesses first published in 1997, is full of expressions of the need to overcome the trauma of Chernobyl in order to recover the evidence and create a narrative about the accident and its aftermath. Amongst the artefacts are the documentaries that have also preserved the conscious awareness of risk as the films were being made. In his 'Monologue on what St Francis preached to the birds', the cameraman Sergey Gurin begins by saying that his experience in the zone around Chernobyl was a secret he had not spoken to anyone about besides his friend (Alexievich 2016: 118–27). He recalls filming a tree in blossom that he couldn't smell, protecting the lens of his camera from the radioactive dust in the country lanes and catching himself 'filming things exactly how I had seen them in the war films'. He tells a story about a rumour that a cameraman had been 'fried', finding out that it was about himself. His traumatic memories of the event are 'a great long film that never got shot'.

The social role of documentary as a window on the truth or as the extension of a heroic or coerced journalistic function is in this way questioned in the aftermath. It is this, perhaps, that characterizes the documentaries about the nuclear industries worldwide after the Cold War. The blind camera, as it was described in one review (Searle 2012), is also a representation of the material objects that have persisted beyond the accident and then beyond the immediate aftermath and which have become the subjects of the contemporary documentaries in this study.

Acknowledgements

I would like to thank the British Academy for support from their small grant scheme to carry out some archive research relating to Chapters 1, 4 and the conclusion. I'd also like to thank colleagues Kathleen Dickson and Steve Tollervey at the British National Film and Television Archive, Jane Harrison at the Royal Institute and Ute Klawitter at the Bundesarchiv in Berlin for their assistance. I am grateful to my colleagues at Surrey University but particularly Bella Honess Roe for her excellent strategy in gaining time to write. My family has turned up trumps with this project so thank you to Sam and Alex Brady for the many explanations and Martin Brady as ever. Finally, my thanks to Faith Newcombe, my anonymous readers and everyone at Intellect Books for all their work.

Introduction:
Risk, reflexivity and documentary film

In 1993, some three years after the fall of the Berlin Wall, Volker Koepp's film *Die Wismut* (*Wismut*, pronounced vissmoot) was premiered at a small documentary film festival in Duisburg. The film begins with a scene outside a small hut in a wood where a group of former uranium miners demonstrates an early procedure for remote underground explosions (Figure 0-1). They use an old company Geiger counter to demonstrate the radioactivity of a mysterious box of ore found from the 1950s and it all ends with a panorama shot over a landscape profoundly changed by the uranium extraction industry. *Wismut* is a modest portrait of a community looking back at the early years of the newly founded German Democratic Republic (GDR). The story is conveyed by survivors, some of whose comrades have died prematurely as a result of working in the mines. As they take the camera crew around various locations, which they wish to preserve to remember their history, they relate how they enthusiastically carried out their physically demanding work to preserve world peace. The storytellers look back on the ideological context and ponder the significance of their own part in it.

Wismut represents in microcosm the central subject of this book. It is one of the first documentary films to engage retrospectively with the social history of the nuclear industries as they developed during the Cold War. Made by a director who was employed by the state for twenty years to film the lives of working people in the GDR, it reflects a wizened and subtle approach to the tricky art of capturing participants in the act of telling their stories. It is a film that could not have been made earlier – the entire region was restricted, and even local residents were not legally permitted to take photographs. It could also not have been made later, as just after the film was finished the remediation process began and both the people and the landscapes began to change.

Wismut is the earliest film in a series of documentaries discussed in this study which explores how contemporary independent documentary filmmakers have approached the subject of the nuclear industries since the end of the Cold War. A central theme within the films is radioactivity. Not usually a visible part of the

1

FIGURE 0.1: Miners demonstrate an early procedure for explosions in the Wismut mines in Saxony, Germany. Volker Koepp (dir.), *Wismut*, 1991, Germany. Südwestfunk, Westdeutscher Rundfunk, ö-film.

film image it is nevertheless the energy that acts as the organizing principle within them. It can be understood as a catalyst for these films – radioactive documentaries – which are prompted by it into making the society of the continuing atomic age more visible. Until the 1990s, social documentary films focusing on the nuclear industries were rare. The classification of information relating to nuclear fission after World War II and caution about advertising the locations and extent of nuclear activities were factors that hid the workforce from view. Although many issues about atomic energy – the morality of the bomb, the vulnerability of nuclear power stations to accidents, the problem of radioactive waste, the links between cancer and radioactive emissions – were extensively discussed in newspapers, on radio and on television from the 1940s into the 1980s, the people engaged in working in industry still remained more or less without a voice, and the places they worked were kept out of bounds. It makes sense then that the period between 1990 and 2016, when the most recent film in this study was made, should have brought forth a number of documentary films on the subject.

Wismut was made by Volker Koepp in the years immediately after the peaceful revolution in the German Democratic Republic. For the newly enlarged Federal

Republic it can be understood as a spontaneous part of a process which took on a more institutionalized form. From 1992 to 1994 labelled 'Working through the history and the consequences of the SED [Socialist Unity Party] dictatorship', and then from 1995 to 1998 'Overcoming the consequences of the SED dictatorship in the process of German unity', the process of understanding and integrating the social history of the GDR has also included Juliane Schütterle's account of life and work in the Wismut SDAG (a company owned jointly by the Soviet Union and the GDR) bringing together interviews with information that was preserved in the archives (Schütterle 2010). Like Schütterle's study, Koepp's film is motivated by the secretive history of the GDR concerning itself with the effects of increased radioactive emissions in this context. Perhaps because of this focus it brings, as I shall argue, a new tone into the exploration of the nuclear industries, representing the first effort at using the particular aesthetics of documentary filmmaking to reflect on rather than argue about the social world of these previously restricted subjects. Thus, although there are special circumstances in this particular case, it is worth taking *Wismut* beyond the specifics of the GDR and comparing it with parallel processes elsewhere in different political contexts.

While the Cold War itself provides one of the relevant historical contexts for the study of these films, the two worst accidents in the history of the nuclear industries, at Chernobyl in Ukraine (then the Soviet Union) in 1986, and Fukushima in Japan in 2011, define its contemporary sense of urgency. Importantly for this study a report published by the Organisation for Economic Co-operation and Development (OECD) ten years after the accident at Chernobyl referred several times to the media as having created negative economic and health effects in their reporting (OECD Nuclear Energy Agency 1995). Calls within the report for better international coordination of information about radiological effects were then repeated in the report of the National Diet of Japan in the wake of the accident at Fukushima in 2011 (The National Diet of Japan Fukushima Nuclear Accident Independent Investigation Commission 2012). Reports on both accidents promoted the idea that the industry would be safer if it were more public, creating the context for increased access globally for independent documentary filmmakers to both the workforce and their places of work. The film *Pripyat* (1999), discussed in Chapter 2, was one of the first in which a documentary film crew was invited to enter the zone around the Chernobyl nuclear power plant to film not only the people guarding it but also the engineers keeping the undamaged reactors in operation, and the people still living nearby. The post-war context, Chernobyl and Fukushima, and radioactivity provide the context for an increase in social documentary films about the nuclear industries.

Documentary film and nuclear technology

A Belgian research group SCK●CEN, which brought together technical and social scientists with humanities research, has been working on the development of a common language for reflection on issues such as the ethics of nuclear technologies, nuclear waste disposal, safety considerations and communication. Alongside the call for the industry to become more accessible to the media is the requirement that the industry develop public consensus about its activities rather than operating solely through internal industry and government decision-making processes. The situation of sites for nuclear waste disposal in particular has become dependent on public consent.

The desire for a degree of mutual understanding between those in the nuclear industries and the general public has not been matched by reality, even though it is asserted in the Belgian report that nuclear culture is coproduced: 'Belgian society shaped the country's nuclear energy provisions, as much as the nuclear energy technology shaped Belgian society itself' (Turcanu et al. 2015: 89). The implications of this idea are difficult to pin down. The group's quantitative studies into media reporting for media research of the nuclear accident at the Fukushima Daiichi plant in Japan analysed choices made about content and aesthetics, but noted that 'media do more than simply provide information about nuclear technology' (Turcanu et al. 2015: 93). The limitations of social and communications research are summed up in the conclusion that points to the possibility of 'a more advanced form of societal decision making that would be prepared to move beyond controversy, and would aim to seek societal trust by its inclusive and deliberative method, rather than by the envisaged or promised outcome' (Turcanu et al. 2015: 95).

This last statement points to the dilemma faced by studies into nuclear communications that inevitably seek to gain social acceptance and cooperation for a controversial technology. The tension between the deliberative methods proposed by SCK●CEN, which are not instrumental, and the authoritarian desire for cooperation, has created out of these reports a paradoxical acceptance of the possibility that the public might simply refuse to give its support. The difficulty in realizing liberal democratic processes is the provocation for much of the documentary filmmaking explored in this book. In a period of expansion for documentary the nuclear theme has proved popular for all kinds of formats, from the teenagers exploring abandoned nuclear power stations in YouTube videos (The Proper People 2019), to the historical drama about the Chernobyl disaster on Sky TV (Renck 2019). Tapping into this interest the documentaries cumulatively represent nuclear energy as it has gradually gone public and in the 30 odd years since the creation of the 'zone of alienation' around Chernobyl, they also represent themselves reflexively as having some agency in the rise of a different kind of nuclear society.

Reflexive modernization and documentary reflection on modernization

The approach taken in each film project to the question of the future in part exemplifies but also in part refutes the reflexivity described by Ulrich Beck in *The Risk Society*, first published in 1986 in which he claimed 'we are eye-witnesses – as subjects and objects – of a break within modernity, which is freeing itself from the contours of the classical industrial society and forging a new form – the (industrial) "risk society"' (1992: 9). The 'break within' is named reflexivity, a critical term that Beck used as part of his analysis to describe the spontaneous appearance of institutions in reaction to the perception of risks produced by industrialisation. Reflexivity is the confrontation of modernity with itself (Beck et al. 1994: 5). Exemplary for this is the case of atomic weapons. In *Risk Society* Beck simply reproduced advice on what to do in the event of an atomic attack to demonstrate the confrontation of nuclear science and industry with itself. He also developed a theory accusing the nuclear industry of developing a myth of scientific infallibility against the spirit of modernity, becoming more entrenched the greater the risk, so that ironically, as he puts it, 'the "safest" thing is ultimately the immeasurable: nuclear bombs and energy with their threats surpassing all concepts and imaginative abilities' (1992: 177). The reflexive process in which the value of technology is put in question and alternatives are tested – which Beck called for as the appropriate response to public protest against nuclear energy in Germany – has proved to be a lengthy and strongly contested struggle. What is more, the struggle over nuclear energy as part of the response to climate change has complicated the picture in complex social ways that become visible in the documentaries discussed in this volume.

Reflexivity, as a positive term to describe the ways in which late modernity might correct itself, is itself problematic, provoking extensive debate during the 1990s, particularly with respect to its relationship with debates around theories of culture. Beck's notion of reflexivity is in conflict with the concept of a social world constructed by its symbols in which self-reflexivity draws attention to the internal contradiction of the text. Beck saw the debate as based on a misunderstanding:

> This concept does not imply (as the adjective 'reflexive' might suggest) *reflection*, but (first) *self-confrontation*. The transition from the industrial to the risk period of modernity occurs undesired, unseen and compulsively in the wake of the autonomized dynamism of modernization, following a pattern of latent side effects.
>
> (Beck 1992: 5)

Reflexive institutions, seeking to deal with problems such as the safe handling of radioactive materials, are not themselves created through reflection. Once created, they seek to deal with the problem. The proliferation of such institutions constitutes the risk society that engages in decision making to reduce risk.

Radioactive documentary could be described as documentary that has moved from the promotion of industrial society – Beck's modernity – to participation in risk society (also labelled second modernity, late modernity or reflexive modernity). For this study Beck's account of reflexive modernity offers a way to understand many developments in documentary. The word 'reflexive' is, however, a complex term within documentary analysis situated between modernist and postmodern debates about culture and society in the second half of the twentieth century. In his *Introduction to Documentary* (2017) Bill Nichols has used 'the reflexive mode' to describe documentary filmmaking that highlights the relationship between filmmakers and audiences. To some extent his use of the term overlaps with Beck's idea of reflexive modernity, in that it can be seen as documentary confronted with its own historical role in promoting industrialization and productivity. That is, in the reflexive mode documentary is challenged by its own tendency to reproduce the established hierarchies of 'traditional' industrial society. It is worth discussing the examples that Nichols chooses. This will then help to contextualize Beck's references to radioactivity as a key phenomenon in making modernity transparent to itself.

The earliest example discussed by Nichols in his introductory account is Dziga Vertov's *Man with a Movie Camera* (1929). He describes the sequence in which the cameraman shoots footage of a horse-drawn carriage followed by the assembly of the film strips in the editing room as deconstructing 'the impression of unimpeded access to reality' (Nichols 2017: 125). Nichols also discusses an example from the 1970s, Jean-Luc Godard and Jean-Pierre Gorin's *Letter to Jane* (1972), in which a journalistic still photograph is exhaustively analysed, confronting image with image to block its transparency. Trinh T. Minh-ha's *Reassemblage* (1992) is a film made by the Vietnamese-born filmmaker with friends from Senegal about a rural Senegalese community. Minh-ha draws attention to the established white and western position of the ethnographic filmmaker by resisting her role as the director of the film, saying that she will 'speak nearby' rather than 'speak about' her subjects. Nichols introduces these films as reflexive at first in an abstract way, equating reflexivity with self-referentiality, which has the effect of somewhat flattening or even distorting the social richness of the films, each of which is inventive with documentary form to make it credible rather than being about documentary itself. Nichols acknowledges this point and goes on to conclude: 'from a political perspective, reflexivity points toward our assumptions and expectations about the historical world more than about film form' (2017: 131).

The social context in which each of these films is reflexive or in the reflexive 'mode' is different. *Man with a Movie Camera* is, as Graham Roberts has argued, a Stalinist film celebrating the establishment of the five-year industrial plan in which the cameraman and the editor are participating (Roberts 2000). Godard and Gorin are engaging in a furious attack on a star for her participation in a celebrity system that renders her efforts to reach out to Vietnamese people flawed and hypocritical. Trinh is perhaps closest to what Nichols is referring to as the reflexive mode, in that she calls the whole act of documentary filmmaking into question. Beck describes reflexivity as a process of confrontation which demonstrates the damage rather than the power of the institution (see Trinh 1993). In Beck's terms the first two films then are modernist affirmations of themselves as progressive films, while *Reassemblage* participates in the language of the reflexive modernization of documentary.

The relationship between reflexivity, self-reflexivity, and reflection in documentary cinema is not fully explained, however, by this notional historicization. What is differentiated with the labelling of these films as modernist, progressive and postmodern is the attitude of the filmmakers to their own roles not the approach to the subject of modernity (celebrated by Vertov, critiqued by Godard and Gorin, rejected by Trinh). Radioactive documentary uses the reflexivity that is spontaneously provoked by the presence of radiation in the image in the same way that Trinh Minh-ha explores the reflexivity spontaneously provoked by the shared experience of the postcolonial condition. As films they do not construct their predicament but are built out of it. It is not the camera in the image that provokes reflexivity but the image in the camera – that is the image of radiation demonstrates the situation of the camera in the radioactive space. If we follow this reasoning through to the three films then Vertov's image of the cameraman places documentary firmly at the centre of modernity. Godard and Gorin claim for their own camera the capacity for reflexive modernization of the media. Minh-ha is engaged in a rejection of documentary as a reflexive part of modernization, suggesting a new way has to be found of using it if it is to have a future. Her act of speaking to one side does not involve reform of the medium but of the relationships that it has institutionalized.

Documentary film, developing alongside other genres in 1930s Britain, has been understood as developing a reflective discursivity about modernity intensifying after World War II in the attempt to create a form capable of enhancing democratic citizenship. Brian Winston, in his book *Claiming the Real* (1995), called into question the capacity of documentary to represent the open and problematic nature of everyday problems by pointing out that documentary producers tended to structure their films with solutions that their sponsors wished to promote. Winston questions the goal of representing reality in the form of documentary, proposing that the purpose of the form should be free, much more diverse and reflexive, capturing ambivalence rather than the certainties of modern progress.

Perhaps counterintuitively then the move of documentary away from reflection – a cognitive activity represented in the expositional mode – towards a reflexive (more direct and emotional) relationship with modernity was only partially achieved through the debates about direct cinema and cinéma vérité. It was the postmodern debates in the 1980s questioning the sources of knowledge that began to confront documentary itself as a modernist institution. Radioactive documentary however marks a return to the reflexive discursivity of non-fiction filmmaking in the post–Cold War period as a delayed development in the case of nuclear culture in Europe, Japan and the United States. In this case self-reflexivity is optional, reinforcing the reflexivity of a radioactive image.

A useful concept that emerges out of the discussion of the difference between 'first' and 'second' modernity is the idea developed by Scott Lash that mediation in second modernity is mimetic. He compares the nineteenth-century novel with cinema:

> If nineteenth-century realist narrative as cultural object is reflexive through highly mediated semiosis, then ideal-typically organized capitalist cinema – in its diachronic, tonal visuality – is a cultural object which is reflexive through less mediated iconic representation. For modes of signification to be less highly mediated (by the subject) is, at the same time, for them to be more highly *motivated* by the phenomenon which is represented. The most proximally mediated, and most highly motivated form of signification, is of course 'signal'.
>
> (Beck et al. 1994: 138)

The engagement in this volume is with documentaries that have approached radioactivity as both a natural and a social subject. The argument here is that the films produce a form of reflexive audiovisuality motivated by radioactivity. What is fascinating about the process is the inhabitation of documentary reflexivity with the physical phenomenon of radiation. The physical environment and the world created by the nuclear industry are reflexive in the social documentary because of the simultaneous action of both the apparatus of filmmaking and radioactivity. The context has not only been created by the safety debates after the accidents at Chernobyl and Fukushima. They also emerge from the continuing questions about radioactive waste management, the decommissioning and remediation of monumental spaces, the capital-intensive economics of nuclear energy and the decarbonization of energy production.

Extending the history of radioactive documentary

The films discussed in this book, beginning with Volker Koepp's *Die Wismut* (1993), have all been made since the end of the Cold War and can be associated with a worldwide will to create greater transparency about nuclear physics and energy production. The list of films extends Eric Barnouw's survey *A History of Documentary* (1993), in which the subject of nuclear energy is discussed in the final chapter entitled 'movement' and is given a generous amount of space. Barnouw himself made a major contribution to the history of nuclear films through the making of *Hiroshima-Nagasaki, August 1945* (1969), a compilation using previously restricted footage. Tracing the scrutiny of the nuclear industry through the politically activist films of the 1970s, Barnouw argued that the topic of radioactive contamination joined the environmental movement in 1989 with the film *Free Zone* (1989) about protests against the transportation of nuclear waste (Barnouw 1993: 306–14). In the same year *Nuclear Free Pacific* gave an account of the Treaty of Raratonga, an agreement signed by thirteen countries of the Pacific to ban nuclear weapons within the zone.

The history of documentary engagement with radioactivity of course began much earlier than the protest films of the late 1960s and earlier even than the restricted US government films produced in the context of nuclear warfare. The way in which footage has been continually re-edited into new non-fiction genres has created a strange coordination between the discovery of contaminated sites and the unearthing of archive film. A film released in 1985 called *Acceptable Risk* about a contaminated site in Canonsburg in the United States, for example, includes footage of Marie Skłodowska Curie visiting the Standard Chemical Company uranium mill in 1921. The history of radioactive photography goes back even earlier than Becquerel's discovery of the phenomenon, to the discovery of X-rays. Akira Lippit has pointed out in his book *Atomic Light* the remarkable way in which 1895, the year that cinema was invented, marked the discovery of the invisible physical and psychic forces, X-rays and psychology. Radioactivity, so named by Curie in a scientific paper published in 1896, was documented through several film genres – industrial, commercial, science, propaganda, and newsreel – before it became relevant to think about the ways in which it was being integrated into everyday life.

A candidate for the first public film about atomic science workers – as opposed to scientists – might be *Atoms at Work*, a British film made by the Crown Film Unit about nuclear isotopes. It begins by stating 'there is no man living who may ignore with impunity what these men do' (the images also show women at work on the atom) and the subject of the film is both the increase in productivity and the ways in which the workers have to adapt to the environment and the radioactive source. There is a case then for investigating further the historical context preceding Barnouw's account of the compilation films protesting against or satirizing government policy on nuclear weapons, including the popular *Atomic Café* (1981), which satirically demonstrates the reflexive quality of atomic bomb films.

As it stands, there is a continuity between the issues outlined in Barnouw's history up to and beyond the accident at Chernobyl power station and the films in this book. At the International Uranium Film Festival, held in various cities across the world each year, contemporary and archive films of all genres are shown addressing them (Uranium Film Festival 2020). In 2018, for example, the film *Chernobyl 3828* directed by Serhiy Zabolotnyi used more archive footage of the soldiers and volunteers as well as an interview with one of the participants to show exactly how the clearing of roofs of the stricken reactor was organized. A Swiss Japanese co-production *The Day the Sun Fell* (2015) is the work of a granddaughter who argues that the silence that followed the accident at TEPCO resembled the same response to Hiroshima. A more light-hearted film called *The Ray Cat Solution* is interesting for the way it picks up the investigations of the US Future Societies researchers to imagine a society oriented around cats that light up in the presence of radiation. Along with archive films, historical questions about the creation and use of atomic weapons are raised. The security threat created by the mere existence of plutonium is explored. The problem of how to store the high level nuclear waste left by the nuclear weapons programmes and by the production of nuclear power is portrayed as increasingly acute as time passes. The safety of nuclear plants for the general public, the health and safety of workers in the nuclear industries, the new problems for land management created by major nuclear accidents, the monitoring of radioactive substances used in nuclear medicine, the use of depleted uranium in new forms of military hardware – all remain issues discussed in the films.

For the feature-length documentary, there is a pivotal transition from the treatment of these themes as part of contemporary issue-based filmmaking to their inclusion in a discovery of a world reorganized by the discovery of radioactivity. As the nuclear industry has reached a new stage in its history, decommissioning and remediation have become a more significant part of its economic activity. This process has coincided with a change in the world order in which understanding and commemorating the past has become intertwined with questions about the impact of human industry on the planet and its future. In this context, films about nuclear energy have shifted ground from being about a movement making arguments against the industry to contemplating the legacy. In keeping with this analysis, the tasks that documentarists have engaged in after the end of the Cold War are markedly different from the establishing years of nuclear weapons and nuclear power, and the years of debate throughout the Cold War, moving instead to the question of how to live with the effects that have built up.

The public discourse to which the films contribute is summarized in a report by *The International Chernobyl Project*, a technical radiological report published by the International Atomic Energy Agency (IAEA) which refers to the concept of safety in radiation contexts as 'especially cryptic' (IAEA 1991: 53). The report states that the radiation protection had not 'fully developed safety criteria for dealing with the type of de facto situations that would be created by widespread contamination following a catastrophic accident'. The most relevant aspect of the report on safety for this book concerns the relevance of 'cultural perspectives, national traditions, social values and professional attitudes'.

> At least three cultural responses to risk are exhibited by western societies: these may be termed pioneering, regulating and moralizing attitudes. [...] These are applicable to the radiation safety community's pattern of response to radiation risk. A pioneering society considers freedom important; it has little concern for risk and in fact is stimulated by risk taking. The regulating society prefers structures and rules; for it, order is most important. For the regulating society, the problem of harmful risks must be solved quantitatively for the sake of order: a value must be clearly set. The moralizing society is strongly motivated by purism, cleanliness and protection. For it, even small risks from any human action are unacceptable, in spite of any derived benefits. Globally, there seems to be a tendency towards the moralizing society, with the associated implications: the pursuit of the 'perfectly safe' technology or the 'absolutely clean' environment.
>
> (IAEA 1991: 53)

The 'moralizing society' as 'second modernity'

Radioactive Documentary focuses on independent social documentary films which generally display the perspective of the 'moralizing society' while encountering pioneering and regulating attitudes. The perception of activities that increase the emissions of radiation as medically harmful is in a sense a prerequisite for reading the films themselves 'radiologically' as materially entangled along with the communities they represent. An important argument about the films is that they represent the lived experience of the participants which is of the pioneering history of nuclear engineering, and the development, maintenance, and improvement of its regulatory regimes. Although protest appears in the films, they are not protest films. The concept of radioactive documentary has to do with understanding the visibility of the relationship between uranium and the social world as one which is mutual.

The films are paired into six chapters addressing (1) the legacy of uranium mining (*Wismut, Uranium Drive-In*), (2) the aftermath of nuclear accidents (*No Man's Zone, Pripyat*), (3) the disposal of high-level nuclear waste (*Into Eternity, Containment*), (4) the closure and decommissioning of nuclear power stations (*Under Control, Indian Point*), (5) the nuclear renaissance (*Pandora's Promise, Return of the Atom*) and (6) the nuclear film archive (*Inside Sellafield, Atomic, Living in Dread and Promise*). Radioactivity itself is the central phenomenon that creates popular interest in these films. What emerges is its social history, its present and its future. As mentioned earlier, the social history of nuclear energy revealed by the radioactive documentary is a mirror or a social correlate of the discovery of radioactivity itself. A notable characteristic of the films to be discussed is that although they display the effects of exposure to radioactivity, inevitably creating a spectacle out of slow disaster, they do not seek to mark out turning points but instead explore how the people involved participate in the ongoing process of living differently, learning in particular to measure, contain, and divert threat.

The films are suggested then as a curated series from 1994 to 2015, a period of a decade and a half that also includes the second most serious global nuclear disaster that took place in Fukushima in March 2011. Each chapter engages with the presence of the camera in the radioactive environment – a reflexive form of social investigation pursued by a team of filmmakers, usually personally motivated by the theme, but also sponsored by others. Following on from this, the communities that are currently emerging in the aftermath of the Cold War are represented and explored.

In Chapter 1, 'Capturing the uranium settlement', the discussion focuses on two films about the contemporary situation for uranium mining and milling communities that formed during the period immediately after World War II. Documentary filmmaking in the German Democratic Republic – the five eastern regions of what is now the Federal Republic of Germany – was known as DEFA documentary and built up a significant and distinctive tradition in association with that label. In the GDR, documentaries played a role as a community resource, engaging with the difficulties experienced by workers which were not generally broadcast on television even though they were sometimes displayed in a controlled way in mainstream fiction filmmaking. In the aftermath of the peaceful revolution, the film *Wismut* is marked by this tradition, but it is also a film that is moving on from it within the new context of the Federal Republic. Participants are in the process of securing their future by reflecting on their past. At the same time the radioactive heritage has become an urgent project that will require extensive investment in sanitation and remediation. The chapter discusses what is shared between this film and the US film *Uranium Drive-In*, taking in particular key scenes in which there is a focus on the measurement of radioactivity in ore. *Uranium Drive-In*, a film about a tiny place called Naturita, Colorado in the United States, which has a history of mining and milling, brings together the divergent memories of people in a community portrayed as visibly divided in public hearings about the proposal to build a new uranium milling facility. The chapter is concerned then with the ways in which uranium ore and its property of radioactivity shows up both reflexively in shots of the landscapes and discursively in the community debates about the past and the future, considering whether they represent the reflexivity of 'second modernity' and if so what kind.

In Chapter 2, 'Framing radioactive sites of evacuation', the significance of measurement becomes more apparent in two documentary films that focus on the meaning of the exclusion zone. The name for the designated area of land varies – it is the zone of alienation in *Pripyat* and no-man's zone in Toshi Fujiwara's film. Nikolaus Geyrhalter and his team were given access to enter the zone around Chernobyl. The film focuses on the radioactive landscape, but the purpose is not to portray the zone as impenetrable. Rather, it is part of a concerted effort to increase public visibility and controlled access. Toshi Fujiwara's *No Man's Zone* (2011), which was a direct response to the Fukushima disaster in 2011, provides a point of comparison. The crew for this film entered the disaster zone before it was declared out of bounds, showing the damage left by the tsunami and interviewing participants who relate what it has been like for them to be evacuated from their homes. Swiftly edited together with a voice-over commentary, the film was conceived in response to media coverage of the accident. In these two films the documentary process provides an opportunity for participants to bring their thoughts to the places that precipitated the global consciousness of radioactivity. The radioactive landscape on-screen is the embodiment of reflexivity: a landscape that is the same yet different. As in Chapter 1 the two films capture an apparently similar situation – the contamination of extensive areas of land with radionuclides – at different stages. The discussion of each film explores how its aesthetic choices work to identify meanings in the decaying buildings and flourishing wildlife particularly as participants are asked to reflect. It is a process that appears designed to instigate a measured process of individual progress in conscious deliberation.

There is a history of journalism and audiovisual representation on the subject of nuclear waste disposal going back to the Flowers report in 1976 which recommended that the development of nuclear power be stalled until this problem could be solved. The theme centres on the search for a location that meets safety requirements and has the consent of the local community. The documentary subject is about creating and maintaining long-term awareness of the effects of a radioactive source at the same time as gaining consent to it. It is thus definitively about the conundrum of reflexive modernity. In Chapter 3 'Placing the nuclear storage site' both films refer to a research project carried out by the United States and published in 1979, which involved an array of experts to consider communication with the distant future. Michael Madsen's *Into Eternity* (2010) takes the problem in a new direction by picking up from the project the effects of time on communication, including in his film representations that convey the fantasy image of the atomic future alongside contemporary images of the landscape and brute rock in Finland in which the waste is to be stored. Peter Galison and Rob Moss's *Containment* (2015) is similarly rooted in the contemporary debate about nuclear waste in the United States. The difference between the two films lies in the fact that Madsen's film is prompted by the dramatic new spaces of Onkalo, the first deep burial site for high-level nuclear waste to be politically agreed and carried out, while Galison and Moss's film is about the rejection of two possible sites in the United States.

The next chapter, 'Remembering the architecture of nuclear power', is concerned with the closure of nuclear power stations as a political and economic effect of the accidents in Chernobyl and Fukushima. Volker Sattel's *Under Control* (2011) collaborates with workers in the German nuclear power industry which is now scheduled to close in 2026, while Ivy Meeropol's *Indian Point* (2016) explores the situation of a single nuclear reactor situated not far from New York. The chapter explores how the films, as radioactive documentaries in the terms of the book, use the context of closure as a moment at which the nature of the nuclear community becomes more visible. At the time the films were made, the decision about closure was being debated, and both demonstrate a strong sense of curiosity about the loss of culture. Volker Sattel's careful national survey recording the spaces and machines of the plants and its staging of safety procedures and workplace rituals is all the more self-conscious because of the planned shutdown. Ivy Meeropol's discussions with the many different participants, who she stages as 'characters' involved in the public debates about Indian Point, build up the social history of the American nuclear everyday. She gains access to scenes within the power station itself where the plant employees believe that greater visibility will lead to greater trust. Both films use opportunities to look around corners as well as to film the pre-arranged events.

Chapter 5, 'New nuclear reflexivity' in contrast, looks at two films concerned with the continued development of nuclear energy technologies. In *Pandora's Promise* (2013) stories of nuclear conversion are told in the conflicted context of the 'nuclear renaissance', a phrase used to describe a period between the millennium and the Fukushima disaster when policy appeared to be turning more generally towards replacing nuclear plants rather than shutting down the industry. The films reflect a complex engagement with reflexive modernity. Mika Taanila and Jussi Eerola's *Return of the Atom* (2015), a satirical documentary about the

Olkiluoto Nuclear Power Plant (OL3), the first nuclear power station to be commissioned in Europe since the accident at Chernobyl, documents the difficulties with many different aspects of the construction project that have delayed its opening. Both films are enacting a defiant response to the accident at Fukushima. *Pandora's Promise* is discussed as a film that attempts to continue with strategies that are no longer valid, constructing a fabricated relationship between uranium and the social world. *Return of the Atom* represents some of the same people who participated in *Into Eternity* but selects interview material and edits it into a collage that draws out the more absurd aspects of the mega project linking it to a more general culture of risk-driven entertainment that the nuclear theme has inspired. The chapter argues that the films exhibit through irony or argument a contorted social history of the nuclear industry.

In the conclusion radioactive documentary returns to the first phase of nuclear development in the form of the storage ponds in one of the UK's first nuclear sites, Sellafield. The highly radioactive artefacts lurking deep under water are shown being brought back up to the surface to be processed and stored more safely. The film represents an almost psychological process of digging up a national nuclear history for reprocessing. It is not accompanied with dread but rather with a matter-of-fact conviction that this legacy can be overcome. As Spencer Weart has argued, the history of representations of radioactivity is consistent in its combination of the emotions of optimistic excitement and fear in response to the idea of transubstantiation (Weart 1988), a vacillation that is both exploited and explored in Mark Cousins' historically cyclical archival compilation *Atomic: Living in Dread and Promise* (2015). Paired with *Inside Sellafield* this work is a film archival version of the storage pond. Made for the seventieth anniversary of the bombings of Hiroshima and Nagasaki, the film explores how the emotions accompanying memory can be therapeutically reorganized not only to acknowledge human suffering properly but also to recognize the complex entanglements involved in scientific and social progress. Nuclear screen culture carries with it an impossibly wide range of emotions.

In radioactive documentaries, the human world is shown as reorganized by uranium. The filmmakers themselves orient their work around it to portray a society that has grown accustomed to this role. They are brought together in this book for the way they contribute to an understanding of the continuing social history of nuclear culture and documentary filmmaking combined. Understood as a modernist machine built to observe and progressively improve cultures of work, the industrial utility of the movie camera is intensified by the discipline of the radioactive environment.

1

Capturing the uranium settlement: Volker Koepp's *Die Wismut* (1993, Germany) and Suzan Baraza's *Uranium Drive-In* (2013, USA)

Introduction

The two films brought together for this chapter offer portraits of participants who remember the communities employed in uranium mining and processing, beginning during World War II in the case of the United States, and at the start of the Cold War in the German Democratic Republic (GDR). Returning to this period the two documentaries acknowledge the secrecy and the questions at that time surrounding the international control of nuclear weapons but are more concerned about the experiences of mining and milling, looking for a social narrative about the nuclear industries. The questions raised by these documentaries now concern the capacity for understanding the Cold War retrospectively. What kind of approach can be taken to the social history of uranium mining and how does it feed in to questions about the industry today? In his book *Slow Violence* Rob Nixon (2013) has brought out the ways in which the drama of apocalyptic narratives has hidden the actual more gradual story of the build-up of toxic industries. Can uranium mining be brought into a more general picture of environmental exploitation during a period that environmental historians have referred to as the great acceleration (McNeill and Engelke 2014), or is there an exceptional story to be told that differs from the toxicity of the chemical industries or from mining for other mineral resources which are not radioactive? Mining and milling is the part of the nuclear industry that was kept most hidden in the early years of the Cold War and the branch that left some of the most severe environmental legacies in the form of tailings ponds and chronic ill health. If the story is exceptional, how does that affect the documentation of the community today?

Volker Koepp's film *Wismut* (1993) was made at the beginning and Suzan Baraza's *Uranium Drive-In* towards the end of the period covered by this survey.

The former is a portrait of a secret mining company first founded in the spa town of Bad Schlema in Saxony, Germany in 1946. The company produced uranium until it was closed down in 1992. *Uranium Drive-In* (2013) is a friendly incursion into a very small community called Naturita in Colorado in the United States. During World War II and the Cold War, the settlements in the area grew along with uranium mining and milling. As part of their engagement with the communities, the films revive the stories shaping the landscape, rescuing them from both the secrecy of the past and the process of forgetting.

Each of the two films enters the story of the community at a new point of upheaval in an existing history of radioactive productivity. In Germany, as part of the process of reunification, a new company, Wismut GmbH, was created in 1990 to close down the mines and sanitize the landscape. In Colorado in 2012, an energy company, encouraged by an apparent upturn in the prospects for nuclear power, proposed opening a new uranium mill. Each film is engaged with radioactivity itself as part of a contemporary sociopolitical context. The study of these films brings out the point that the media production contexts in which they were made are worth discussing in themselves as they both in some sense test the capacities of documentary as a means of intervention in social life. Who the filmmakers are and how they came to be involved in creating their images of the landscapes and communities shaped by radioactivity forms part of the understanding of them as part of the phenomenon, the 'toxic camera' moving from the images of contaminated spaces to the organization of society around them.

Following on from the identity of the producers is the motivation of the participants in making the films. Here the two films differ in an interesting way. For *Wismut*, a particular group, the veterans or the 'aristocracy' who are first-generation survivors significantly shape the narrative, clearly motivated by the desire to tell their story. They are not the only voices, however, as others are brought in offering different perspectives that demonstrate the particularity of the veterans' experience. Nevertheless the story begins and ends with them. There is a less clearly identifiable core group in *Uranium Drive-In* which spans more than one generation. As each group is considered, its position is shown to be valid, fulfilling the educational aim of the film to provide an opportunity for more meaningful dialogue about the future.

The reflexive point to bring out of the discussion concerns the reorientation of the communities around the history rather than the presence of uranium mining. Both films are engaged at a point where the vulnerability of social organization around it is exposed. The finite nature of mineral extraction is not unique to these communities but the radioactive legacy maintains a different kind of presence of the past. Thus the fact that the town at the heart of *Uranium Drive-In* was completely destroyed as part of the sanitation of the land during the 1980s might be understood as an attempt to make the past disappear that fails because of the lack of a replacement economy. In contrast, the ambitious goal of Wismut GmbH – as has unfolded since the making of *Wismut* – was to restore the landscape to use for leisure and renewable energy and to return places such as Bad Schlema to spa town status.

The legacy of the DEFA documentary

As with Shevchenko's *Chernobyl: A Chronicle of Difficult Weeks*, Koepp's film about the world of the Wismut mines came at a moment of ideological change, making it part of a new and unaccustomed openness. While Shevchenko was engaged in capturing a dynamic situation as it unfolded, Koepp filmed a moment at which an industry had wound down.

In 1993 *Wismut* was already the sixth film Volker Koepp had completed in the new larger Federal Republic of Germany. Like many films made in the wake of reunification it can be interpreted first and foremost as an act of communication, informing people in the west of Germany and in the wider world that the company had existed.

At the same time that the uranium mines were privatized to form Wismut GmbH, the DEFA film studios of the GDR were also being wound up. Up until 1992 Koepp had belonged to a group called 'document' within the DEFA Studio for Newsreel and Documentary Films. Regarded as a relatively harmless form of filmmaking – so long as it was not broadcast on television – documentary filmmaking developed in the GDR into a distinctive form of cinéma vérité. Films were made in the workplace in an observational style with little voice-over commentary and a consistent visible presence of the camera crew (Schreiber 1996). Cinematographers worked with 35-mm black-and-white film stock that, while much less expensive than the colour stock used for higher prestige forms, had a special quality. The films had a much more static feel than the more mobile 16-mm cameras used in the West, which added to the sense of the GDR as a historic experiment even as it was failing right up to the end of the 1980s (Schreiber 1996). When it came to the protests in Leipzig, Berlin and Dresden filmmakers such as Gerd Kroske and Andreas Voigt used the same cameras and observational style with the same black-and-white film stock.

Although DEFA continued to produce films, sometimes continuing long-term projects or reviving previously suppressed productions, it was finally closed by the *Treuhandanstalt,* an agency trust set up to privatize or wind down the nationalized companies in the GDR. In 1992 some members of the group had already started an independent workshop named 117 with the aim of continuing their documentary filmmaking tradition. Koepp managed to make films with different production companies being set up at the time and was assisted in making *Wismut* by Katrin Schlösser and Frank Löprich, also former DEFA filmmakers, who formed the production company ÖFilm (playing on the common ö in their names) (Hecht 1996).

Koepp (whose name is also a variant on the ö theme) was able to continue partly because the brand of documentary filmmaking he had developed as a film-maker for twenty years in the GDR turned out to be highly suited to conditions in the Federal Republic. His focus on the long-term relationships between people and the history of place in particular became even more significant through the historic events leading up to the fall of the Wall in 1989, the reunification of Germany in 1990, and the creation of the five new *Bundesländer* or Federal States. His long-term projects observing particular communities and individuals gained a new resonance and he was also able to explore new territories such as with his first international success after reunification with the East Prussian film *Kalte Heimat* (*Cold Homeland* 1995a).

Koepp's style of filmmaking, with its focus on people in the GDR is also particu-larly suited to an exploration of a radioactive landscape. As his participants speak about their experiences, the camera discovers the relationships between their move-ments in the space and the environment. Sometimes it can be about a sense of being at home but more often it is about a desire to be somewhere else, or to change a frustrating situation. *Wismut* is shot by Thomas Plenart, a long-time collabora-tor of Koepp who recorded the participants, their clothing, their coiffeur, their gestures, as signifiers of a time and a place. Looking back at it from 2019 it is a record of a mood as the participants ask themselves what the meaning of the Cold War was. Such was the importance of this question, the film was supported in this effort by the Federal Ministry of the Interior's film fund, by the Berlin and Saxon film funds, as well as by three different German television channels.

A history of banned images

In an account of his filmmaking before 1990 Koepp described the GDR film company DEFA as a 'corset' because of the refusal to allow a realistic representa-tion of life in the GDR. When it came to the Wismut mines, this suppression was extreme. In the late 1950s Konrad Wolf attempted to represent the foundational period of the mines as a realist depiction of the difficult early years of the GDR in his film *Sonnensucher* (*Sun Seekers*, 1958). The film portrays former prisoners and Nazi party members brought together with convinced communists all serving under benign but tough soviet leaders. In the film they struggle with each other and the rock to establish peace by contributing to the building of the atom bomb.

For all its strong message about the foundation of the GDR against all odds, and its consultation with miners about its representational strategies, the film was withdrawn by Soviet censors in the context of complaints from the company and heightened tensions with the United States. It was given a limited release in 1972.

The intensity of the period was also expressed in a banned novel *Rummelplatz* (*Fairground*) written by Werner Bräunig, who conveyed the world of the Wismut company through a story of conversion to socialism as the building of strength and resilience. One character called Christian who has been assisting comes to the point where he becomes a driller, the highest paid level of worker in the mine. Bräunig describes his gradual acclimatization to his task until he comes to a revelation:

> The work overcame him like an addiction, suddenly and overwhelmingly. He inserted the drill bit and pushed it with all his strength into the mountain, the force of the compressed air shook his body, the kick back went like a shudder through his flesh and made his muscles taut. Christian felt the rhythm of the work. Now the mountain was releasing all its secrets.
>
> (Bräunig 2015: 115)

Although this work had been developed in the context of the Socialist Unity Party and the 'Bitterfelder Weg', a literary movement that supported workers in their writing about their working life, it was refused publication. The state newspaper *Neues Deutschland* published an article on 7th December 1965 attacking Bräunig for his false representations of the wild lifestyle of its protagonists. As the author Christa Wolf wrote in a foreword to an edition of the novel published in 2007, Bräunig never produced another book and died of alcoholism at the age of 48.

Even a television series starring Armin-Müller-Stahl, *Columbus 64*, about a young journalist and writer with bourgeois tendencies – and who is educated by his experiences as a Wismut lorry driver into becoming a good worker, faithful husband, attentive father, and committed citizen – was shown just once in 1966 with cuts. After the last episode, despite many positive reviews, the GDR television company DFF received many letters complaining about the portrayal of Wismut workers, which Paul Wagner has interpreted as part of an organized campaign on the part of the company against any more broadcasts (Wagner 2012).

The filming of *Wismut* hence represents the incursion of the camera into a landscape that has been programmatically withheld from the public gaze. The hollowed-out landscapes, slag heaps and tunnels represent the effects of a huge effort over forty years. In his popular history *Uran für Moskau* (Uranium for Moscow) Rainer Karlsch has written that the real scandal of the Wismut company was the complete failure of the GDR government to respond to the environmental issues. In answer to the question as to why, Karlsch points first to suppression and then to extensive falsification of the environmental data by the Secretary of State for the Economy, in a position second only to the party leader. The importance of the income from the mines had become so great that, Karlsch argues, the ministers for the environment and for water were kept ignorant of the realities of the situation. As a result housing was situated next to radioactive slag heaps and water was declared safe to drink. Karlsch concludes that in the small inner group: 'environmental pollution was regarded as the "price of progress", "an unavoidable evil", or even as the "price of the struggle for peace"' (Karlsch 2011: 193–95).

In 1992 when Koepp was shooting the film, the Federal Republic had, as part of international agreements with the USSR, accepted full responsibility for the company and its liabilities and was just beginning an extensive programme to survey the land and begin with the process of sanitation. The film cannot be said to be primarily about environmental protest any more or about the politics of reunification. Rather, after these moments of major historical change, the film's achievement is to have captured some of the physical locations of the company at the beginning of a long remediation process, and to have interviewed some of the longest serving of the employees who had lived within its regime. At a moment of transition, the participants in the film tell their stories. Some reflect on their sense of having been rescued from destitution while others recount the miners' exposure to health risks, particularly in the first years after the war. As the first feature documentary about atomic energy in the GDR to reach an audience in the post-Cold War era, the film is also one of the first to start to situate its story explicitly within the broader historical narrative from 1946 to 1989.

The sound and image of Wismut radioactivity

At the time of Koepp's film, the participants are already well versed in conveying to younger generations the long history of mining which in Saxony goes back to the sixteenth century. There was an exhibition mine and museum during the1970s that showed visitors how early miners in Johanngeorgenstadt, a central location for the film, went about their work. There is no mention in the film that this town right on the border with Czechoslovakia had become one of the routes through which the people had started to leave the GDR before the border with West Germany was opened. The film is not about the recent politics, although this is the context for the people interviewed. Instead it focuses completely on the act of remembering, looking back. Its focus is also not on the entire history of the uranium mines that lasted from the closing stages of World War II to closure in 1991. The participants talk in the main about the first period as the *Ostzone* became the GDR and as the old silver, tin and bismuth mines were adapted to the larger scale of uranium extraction. The 'aristocracy' who are the focus are those who are still alive to tell the stories of those times.

There is, then, an interesting oscillation in the film between the radioactivity of the past and that of the present. Clearly there is no difference between the two except that the central group is concerned with remembering radioactivity in the past rather than with thinking about its presence. While the participants carry out the routine described at the beginning of the introduction to this book, one miner blows on a trumpet, a historical artefact in itself, another detonates some explosive 40 metres below in a shaft beneath a shack, it becomes clear that the film crew remain aware of the radioactive ore (see Figure 1.1). 'Tell us about this box', says the director. The participant, who reappears at several points in the film, is practised at talking about this box of uranium ore, or pitchblende, handling its contents while speaking. He demonstrates its radioactivity using an embossed SDAG Wismut company Geiger counter. The ore, he explains, is from the 1950s, inexplicably found in a metal box in a tunnel called 'nameless'. It would have been very valuable back then, but now 'nobody wants it anymore' (Koepp, *Die Wismut*, 1994). In the course of the forty-plus years since it was left behind, the ore has developed uranocite on its surface, a beautiful glittering mineral that glows under UV light, which the camera shows in a close-up of the surface of the rock. He also mentions that the box would have earned the miner a good sum of money at the time.

FIGURE 1.1: A demonstration of the radioactivity of uranium ore using original Wismut equipment in Saxony, Germany, Volker Koepp (dir.), *Wismut*, 1991. Germany. Südwestfunk, Westdeutscher Rundfunk, ö-film.

The demonstration of radioactivity is carried out in a highly transparent style, typical for the cinéma vérité film, moving the camera from the counter to the reading and showing the sound from the headphones being picked up by the microphone. As the participants and the filmmakers know, this exercise in imagining how things were done is already becoming an increasing part of the future for the region as it turns away from uranium production to tourism and the recreation of the radium spa resorts that existed in the early twentieth century. But as he handles the ore he does not wear gloves or protect his hands from the rock in any way, raising a question about the radioactivity that has just been demonstrated. As the instrument produces the classic crackling sound, the ore is described as 'whistling', a local term to indicate the presence of the ore, and the monitor moves from zero to the top of the range. The camera moves in close-up over the instrument showing embossed on the metal 'SDAG Wismut WTZ Unirad-Z 6590' giving some very exact information about what it was and when it was issued.

How should this sequence be understood? It is not possible for a general audience at this point in the film to draw any conclusions about the ore other than that it is radioactive. The implication of the increasingly loud 'whistling', the statement of the presenter that it is 'high quality ore', and the fact that the scale appears to be switched to the highest reading set up some of the conflicting information for the viewer between the behaviour of the presenter and the message of his machine. The film leaves this hanging, however, and moves instead to a charming sequence of close-up shots on a piece of folk art accompanied by the mining song *Glück Auf* performed by a traditional male voice choir. A mechanical model of a snowy mountain above a mine complete with skiers, miners and drillers with headlamps ends with a skeleton emerging from a misty hollow.

While the small shack in the woods creates a vision of an artisanal activity on a small scale, a new location in a vast open cast mine shows a space that will eventually be partially filled with slag and refunctioned. A lorry is driven into the space, giving a sense of scale as the camera pans across from the valley leading into the quarry and then turns until it rests on the scene.

It is not until the third radioactive location that the questions left hanging in the first are resolved. The crew are conveyed down to a complex of tunnels, and a collage of shots following the workings of the machinery shows how they travel through the dark and dripping spaces. Whitewash along the way reveals the office and places where the men rest. Some more 'splendid ore' is brought forth and a miner brings out a Geiger counter in the shape of a tube to demonstrate how it is used. This time, however, his headphones are not recorded and Koepp asks the question 'isn't it dangerous? One imagines…'.

These scenes hide to reveal. Writing about the films of the former GDR, including those that were made just after reunification, Schweintz et al. have discussed the kind of evidence documentary films provide in the writing of history, pointing

FIGURE 1.2: A former open-cast uranium mine in Thuringia, Volker Koepp (dir.), *Wismut*, 1991. Germany. Südwestfunk, Westdeutscher Rundfunk, ö-film.

out that although the films store information they also store ways of seeing events and determine what is forgotten as irrelevant as well as what is remembered as important (Ebbrecht et al. 2009: 7). Revelation in the documentary film narrative is a constructed event, of course it could not be otherwise. Even the flashes of light in *Chernobyl: A Chronicle of Difficult Weeks* construct its moment of realization and horror. Is it then a revelation at all? After all, some people will know already that uranium ore is weakly radioactive, that it gives off 'alpha' radiation, easily deflected by a sheet of paper or a tee-shirt, so weak it will not travel very far from the rock itself. Should this documentary film be seen as merely participating in the presentation of the uranium mine as tourist resort? Is it aimed at people who come to learn about its history and to dispel the myths and the legends? Or is this a preliminary stage in a radiological search for more truths revealed as part of the film and the measurements provided by instrumentation? For historians documentary film is a source of images to support mediated memories, to represent 'ways of thinking and ideologies that have become historical' (Ebbrecht et al. 2009: 7), but it is also the case that compilation films, observational documentaries and historical compilation films stage documentary material historically to construct memories retrospectively for reflection at a particular moment in time.

Shot in black and white the film stock itself of *Wismut* historicizes the mine along with the re-enactments offered by the participants who stage it as a radioactive place for presentation and for explanation. The uranium ore brought to demonstrate the old practices is emitting alpha particles so that radioactivity can become an explicit part of the filming. The headphones are shown to make the link. When the filmmaker asks the miner about his thoughts about his work, however, he resists framing himself historically within a chain of causation that defines his life and his identity as damaged. He does not present himself as a survivor or witness providing testimony to record his experiences to generate sympathy in his audiences, as theorists such as Sarkar and Walker have defined such audiovisual testimony. Not seeing himself as contaminated he asserts the difference between the military use to which the product of his work was put and plays down the effects of radiation on miners saying they were aware of the risks.

A Geigercounter?
Yes. With this tube we can see if there is any ore there. It is shaped to go into a bore hole. A meter and a half or so in.
And it is not dangerous?
It depends. This is not the kind of radiation released at Hiroshima. It is weaker. It can be stopped by my tee-shirt. The decay products are dangerous though. Radon gas has no smell, no taste and is colourless.
And did you have any second thoughts?
Why should I? I am a miner. This is how I earn a living. And so you have to live with it. We all know it is not a chocolate factory. And the damaging effects are not so common in this particular role.
It is more dangerous processed?
When it is processed yes. And in the form of bombs it is totally dangerous.

This exchange sets up a challenge to the idea that the company Wismut was anything extraordinary. It normalizes the radioactive quality of the ore and represents it as an ordinary product of industry. The hazards – the radon gas particularly – are presented as known and controllable and the military use is acknowledged, but it is sceptical about the interest shown by the filmmakers. The revelation is a Wizard of Oz experience, the crackling Geiger counter as acousmatic sound.

And so there is something to learn about the transition of radioactivity from health and safety issue to historical artefact. *Wismut* is a radioactive documentary of its own time, an expression of the transition from the 'state within a state' intent on production to the new corporation dedicated solely to land remediation. The tension brought out by the focus on radioactivity in the film is able to divide the gaze between the invisible threat and the organization of the space around extraction. The movement of the camera around the detail of the machinery and the spaces is both a constant search for functional connections between cables, cogs, carriages, cabins, and a representation of the history of the people's own company. The Geiger counter, which was also shown in some detail in the first scene, is now a popular collector's item, so it is possible to find out that model Z was used by the Wismut geophysicists or the workers trained to look for uranium ore. As the miner in the third scene explains, the shape of the tube is designed to fit into a drill hole to detect the presence of radioactivity and follow the seam. The close-up on the different scales on the monitor in the first scene translates into readings measured in microröntgen per hour. The reading, 40,000 μR/h, we see on the Geiger counter, does not represent a health hazard up in the fresh air and even down in the mineshaft as the particles are too weak to reach the miner, as he explains. The possibility of detecting the ore this way, however, has enabled its extraction. The shape of the tube mirrors the shape of the tunnel. The film begins to reflect the meaning of the radioactive crackle as a larger exploration into the knowledge that the men have as part of their experience and which they are imparting in the aftermath of their company's time in operation. As the film progresses, the sound of radioactivity comes to represent the social and environmental transformation around it.

Radioactive society

Thus, while the ore is not radioactive in a way that creates a health hazard in these scenes, one of its decay products, radon gas (which presents a radiological problem across many parts of Europe) is mentioned in several scenes. As the participants explain the problem to the filmmakers, including the rates of emission in terms of becquerels per cubic metre, the camera scans the space around them turning it once again into a radioactive scene. Below ground, two of the participants explain the extent of the tunnelling where the mines are being sealed to prevent radon gas emissions. The film creates a three dimensional sense of the movement of radioactivity around the space. Above ground, a woman explains her life history, coming to the region with her father shortly after the war, and as the discussion turns to the use of the empty buildings around her, her reticent account erupts into emphatic scorn over the naivety of prospective tenants who are not aware that the entire region is contaminated. 'We heard the explosions below in our beds at night', she explains. Meanwhile, the headlamps of the miners in the space below create a white halo in the inky black darkness.

Radon gas is a public health hazard in many regions in the world. Uranium atoms are present in many different kinds of geology and decay at a steady rate, transmuting into other elements including the noble gas radon that can collect in houses as it is emitted from the ground. The engaged and informed way in which the participants in the film explain the issues counteracts the mystery of the scenes of the opening in a key move for radioactive documentary after the Cold War. The language about radioactivity is not emotive here but factual. The landscape and its invisible emissions of alpha particles is part of the everyday, shifting the invisible threat to the tunnels crisscrossing beneath the ground 'like a piece of cheese'. Gradually, it is the shifting of rock that becomes recognizable as the mark of the new, a geological era marked by human presence now referred to as the Anthropocene. Johanngeorgenstadt, an old town now on the border with the Czech Republic, is on top of a hill below which the mine shafts rose up to the centre of the town. In the end the buildings above had to be destroyed. Today there are still visible signs put there by the community demanding the restoration of the buildings and compensation for their loss.

The shift between the invisible aura of radioactivity and the visible effects of extraction is mirrored in the stories relating to health. The *Schneeberger Krankheit* (lit. snow mountain illness) is one of the earliest recorded names given to lung cancer, first noted at the end of the fifteenth century in the silver mines in the Erzgebirge. Even then this mysterious illness did not affect as many miners as silicosis. Several of the participants in the film explain their experience of seeing their fathers as invalids at a young age. A group of radiological experts from the company takes the filmmakers through the statistics concerning the acknowledged health damage to thousands of workers. Creating a striking image for this hazard, the participants in the film demonstrate dry drilling, showing the dust envelop them in the halo of light shining from their headlamps.

The measured society

As the participant workers tell their Cold War stories, however, the tone changes again with strong variations in the emotions expressed about historical radioactivity. An ambivalence enters into the account developed by the film, which becomes complicit in recreating the sense of the community lured into dependence. 'We shouldn't be so bitter', says one man, displaying the minerals he has collected during his career. 'The money was good'. In key scenes in the film the participants talk about the period before 1950 which they humorously label the *Gründerzeit*, a reference to the period of industrial development before the Unification of Germany in 1871. The oldest member, who they claim was the third worker to join the mine, having been given the number three, describes his own zeal about mining uranium for peace.

Koepp accompanies their accounts with photographs that provide evidence of the arrival of thousands of men and also a number of women to fulfil the task of providing uranium ore. One participant with such a history describes his own life story as one of progress as he rose up from the bottom through the ranks of the company, gaining a university education, and going on to work in an office at the company headquarters. The intensity and the pride in the work echoes Werner Bräunig's novel, mentioned above. The stories emerge in the context of different social gatherings filmed and edited in a sequence covering the high security of the mines with barbed wire and dogs, the designation of the region as closed, the heavy and demanding nature of the work, the poor health conditions along with the increase in provisions – all of which is evidenced through artefacts such as identity papers, photographs of overcrowded trains and locations where the miners lived and drank together. The editing of the material ensures a level of realism through balancing the more sentimental statements about the past and the solidarity of the miners against other witness accounts that point to threatening group behaviour, bullying and incompetence. At several points in the film there are examples of folk art, particularly models of mountain landscapes showing the mines beneath the surface with their animated wagons and figures. A sequence in which the miners' song, the *Steigerlied* with its opening greeting *Glück auf, glück auf!* is sung by a group of former miners in the station in Johanngeorgenstadt is followed by another in which women who worked for the company talk about their lower pay, enduring foul language and their difficulty getting onto the trains and buses to work. One of the women, who worked as a lorry driver and as a radiographer, describes how she once had to strip naked on leaving the mine only to discover that she was showing up as radioactive because of the dust in her hair. Koepp finds people who did not choose to go and work in the mines despite the attractive pay. At the centre of the film one of his 'aristocrats' states that after long years of illness, the death of his brother and his best friend, and his persistent study of the historical background to the uranium mines, he believes that it was not necessary and especially not worth the terrible damage done to the environment.

In the aftermath of such conditions, extended well beyond the fifties up until the demise of the GDR, the film shows how radioactivity drew in resources and camouflaged indifference to health and social well-being. It is ironic then that as the region has been rehabilitated environmentally, it has become important for the broader population not to stigmatize the area for its past by focusing unduly on the threat of radiation. The revelation offered by the film is that the secretive world created by the Cold War race to build the atom bomb was enabled by the idea that anything to do with uranium, not just its military applications, was to be restricted and kept out of the public gaze. In effect radioactivity provided an invisible cloak. The lifting of the restrictions to image making, however, has a double edge. While radioactivity provides an aura, it also signals a threat. The radioactive documentary, then, is importantly not only safe in the cinema but also indicates the historicity of the threat in the landscapes represented too.

The society of measurement

Since Koepp's film many more have appeared in the context of Die Wismut GmbH and its regeneration of the region. Extensive documentation about the history of the mines and their condition at the end of the GDR as well as about the sanitation of the area has been carried out by two former GDR documentary filmmakers Joachim Tschirner and Burghard Drachsel. Their first documentation *terra incognita: Die Wismut* (Unknown Territory: Wismut) was made for the *Bundesgartenschau*, a huge national biennial horticultural show that was held in the remediated towns and landscapes of Gera and Ronneburg in 2007, to reassure visitors that they would not be exposed to higher levels of radioactivity in the region than elsewhere in Germany. In their more recent second documentary, they nevertheless describe the sanitation of the water as a 'task for eternity' (Tschirner and Drachsel 2016). A former miner employed in the regeneration project states:

> An important lesson learned for us as miners, and particularly for the Wismut company, was that nature cannot be endlessly violated because it is a long process to heal the wounds, a process which requires very high financial costs. This in itself must make us more protective of the environment. This, I believe, is the most important thing that we have learned from the process of sanitation for the future. We must communicate this to the generations to come, that we need to treat nature softly and gently.
>
> (Tschirner and Drachsel 2007)

In 1993 as a model of cultural memory, *Wismut* was engaged in an important way with a transition for the people in the landscapes created by uranium mining. Koepp used the old techniques of filmmaking during the DEFA period when documentary films that represented local problems were taken from place to place rather than broadcast on television. The film captures a sense of forced solidarity amongst the miners that is familiar to Koepp from his own experiences with the state film studio DEFA, about which he wrote:

The limited space had its advantages. We knew the people, we had similar sorrows, similar joys, we knew the landscapes, cities, villages. We could meet people more than once. What looks like an insider job [...] is of course because a group of people – forced to be together in DEFA – sometimes friends, sometimes enemies, had very similar experiences in life, the same CVs.

(Koepp 1995)

There is surprisingly little landscape photography in the film, given Koepp's reputation as a landscape filmmaker, but towards the end the gigantic slag heaps with their characteristic conical shapes are shown covered in snow. The film ends with a peeping Geiger counter measuring the road which appears to have been made with uranium ore and continues to sound over the final and first open panoramic landscape shot that follows.

The camera at the Uranium Drive-In

It puts this German documentary in a wider global context to explore how the environmental and social issues raised by the history of uranium mining are represented on the other side of the ideological conflict. *Uranium Drive-In* is a film made some twenty years after *Wismut*, introducing a documentary camera into a tiny community in Colorado in the United States arguing about building a new uranium mill at a site nearby. It was in development over two years from 2010, covering the period just before and just after the accident at Fukushima Daiichi Nuclear power station in March 2011. President Barack Obama supported the development of the nuclear energy industry in 2010 with the creation of a government loan guarantee to companies developing new nuclear reactors (Goldenberg 2010). For the mayor of the poverty-stricken town where some families were struggling to feed and clothe their children, the mill represented the possibility of economic survival. The portrait of the positive community response to the reintroduction of a uranium mill draws out not only the circumstances of climate change as a positive driver for a renewal of nuclear energy, but also the economic circumstances of the communities that were left behind after the industry folded.

Uranium Drive-In is a twenty-first-century film driven by an independent documentary filmmaker supported by many different funders. The film was distributed through several different outlets. Although small, the distributor Journeyman Pictures has links to the global media distributors Apple, Google and Amazon as well as through an educational distributor New Day Films. The educational purpose of the film was supported by teaching materials to guide discussion with a particular focus on the economy of small rural communities (Reel Thing 2013). The network of interested agents that participated in the film and helped fund it is also broad.

Funding came from private donors and charitable foundations including support-
ers of environmental groups, of educational initiatives as well as the political
figures Bill Clinton and Barack Obama. The Sundance Institute Documentary Film
Programme and Fund also supported the film. All these clearly place the film as a
Democrat-backed piece promoting deliberation.

The history of radioactivity emerges as one among a number of competing
narratives inserted through different media. One narrative relates to the tradition
of uranium mining in the area. Film extracts from *The Petrified River* (1956) made
by the Bureau of Mines and Union Carbide demonstrate how the United States
was advertising its development of nuclear power and weapons in the mid-1950s
while the GDR was suppressing all reference to it. As in *Wismut*, the community
that has formed around the industry is portrayed as having historically adapted to
the nature of the radioactive source, providing a knowledgeable workforce and an
informed and aware broader community. As he pitches the mill to the community,
the CEO of Energy Fuels states that he doesn't need to tell the community what
the opening of a new mill will mean. The mayor is introduced as a member of the
community who is enthusiastic about the promised revival of the town's ailing
economy. The proposed Piñon Mill which will 'give us life again' is welcomed by
the local people with applause. Wrapped around the local narrative and at first
supporting it is a national one in which President Barack Obama declares the
important role of nuclear energy for the future, promising reconnection between
the economy of this remote region and the national grid.

Reviewing the radioactive past

While *Wismut* in 1992 was able to film the first generation of uranium miners after
World War II, *Uranium Drive-In* interviews a group of women who meet and tell
the story of how they moved to Uravan as children with their parents who were
uranium workers. One story captures the ambivalent manner of all of the women
particularly well, as she recounts her youthful admiration of the colours in the
river bed, not knowing they were caused by toxic waste products. Amateur 8-mm
video footage of the town of Uravan, set off as a projected frame within a frame
and accompanied by the sound of a small projector, provides visual evidence for
the women's memories of growing up in the disappeared town. Their commentary
voiced over the digitized footage creates a new radioactive media artefact out of
the old one, turning it into a composite image of childhood ignorance and adult
awareness of the meaning of contamination.

Again like *Wismut* the film is also concerned with documenting the radioactive
sites of the present as they have persisted from the past. One of the women takes the
filmmakers to the location where Uravan was once situated. The image is framed
full of hazard signs indicating it is a restricted area even though the area it has

FIGURE 1.3: A frame from an amateur film showing children playing in the lost town of Uravan is incorporated into the story, Susan Beraza (dir.), *Uranium Drive-In*, 2013. United States. Reel Thing.

already undergone a sanitation. After this moment of mourning for a town, the film moves to other testimonies relating to the mines and the Cañon City, Cotter Corporation Uranium Mill, now a Superfund site containing a large tailings pond which is decommissioned and due to be sanitized. Two participants suffering ill health – one a worker who was involved in an accident and covered with refined uranium ore and the other a miner invalided with pulmonary fibrosis – are living representations of the risks posed by the industry. In keeping with the balance of the film one of them sees the risks as unacceptable and the other sees them as having been overcome by modernized technologies. The miner is supported by an organization called the 'Cold War Patriots' – helping those who worked in the uranium industries during the Cold War – and the nurse who tends him clearly also presents a positive narrative that helps in terms of the psychology of his illness.[1] Here is where the sequence brings in a twist with respect to the debate as a whole as one of the former miners asserts that contemporary mining and milling should not be compared with the conditions endured during and immediately after the war.[2]

Toxic camera

Out of all of the scenes in the film a visit to the rusting scaffolding of a former mine used as a nuclear waste dump brings out the in situ quality of the radioactive documentary most clearly. The visit includes a Geiger counter placed on a pile of rock on the outside of the disused uranium mine. The camera shows a reading in close-up of 7.8 μSv rising to 8.56 μSv. As mentioned in the introduction this is a medical reading about the dose that would be absorbed by the body in one hour in the place where the Geiger counter is located. Making this measurement marks a significant change in individual behaviour and the beginning of an engagement in the process of calculation that is normally left to experts. There are by now many websites with information presented at various levels of complexity explaining what the average dose on a normal day might be, what the dose a flight across the Atlantic would involve or the doses from various types of medical imaging. In *Uranium Drive-In* this kind of information is not conveyed however and as in *Wismut* the number is simply left hanging.[3]

Before moving on to the nuclear accident at the Fukushima Daiichi plant in Japan, which not only changed public perception but also promoted the production of more accessible information, it is worth pausing at this scene. The focus on radioactivity here is about more than the question of how many microsieverts per hour are recorded. It is more about a transition from a society that is not conscious of the environment in this way, to a society that is. The act of measuring is defined in a technocratic society by role but in democratic societies the definition of expertise that comes with this role has been changing. In the 1990s Chaia Heller picked up on the changing definition of expertise in the context of food and the environment, arguing that the *paysan* became a significant bearer of relevant knowledge in the debate about genetically modified crops (Heller 2004). In the case of activism and the nuclear industry, the measurement of radioactivity by experts employed by campaigners is a symbol for taking on the task of discovering the facts. This process has developed a step further, however, and in the context of this documentary this act is not presented as part of an argument but rather to show a social change. It shows that anyone can invest resources in making personal measurements of the environments relevant to them.

In the course of filming, the plan to build the new mill is halted by the nuclear accident in Japan so that the documentary has now become a record of the way in which the nuclear renaissance stalled. By the end of the film the new mill was not being built but for economic reasons rather than because of local resistance. As the film has not really been about putting the case for or against this outcome, it returns it to the social circumstances of the new millennium, the scarcity of work nearby, the effects on family life of long commuting times, unemployment, dependence on state aid for medical care and food. Although the participants in the film state that they recognize the risks, like the participants in *Wismut* they are also realistic about the quality of life.

Uranium Drive-In is not a film about the history of atomic energy in the United States but about the current situation of the people living in the settlements that grew during the Cold War. Although the dismantling and removal of the entire town of Uravan with its impressive cost of $120 m appeared to mark the end of a period, the continued maintenance of the land marked as contaminated indicates the continuing presence of its history not only in the memories of those who grew up there but also in the remaining toxic chemicals that cannot be easily removed. In its exploration of the social disturbance caused by the proposal to build a new uranium mill, Baraza's film turns the documentary into an active community resource – as does Koepp's *Wismut* – which recognizes the role of history and memory in the construction of the future. As such, bringing the films together draws out some striking similarities in the understanding of the early years of the Cold War.

Situated testimony

Janet Walker has suggested a 'social ecological' reading of documentary films that grapple with cases combining complex social and historical factors with the effects of environmental disaster (2010: 94). Walker's analysis is concerned with subjects who return to a place they have been forced to leave by an environmental disaster and who in their testimony reconnect with sometimes traumatic memories. Her question is concerned with the 'right to return' that is disrupted by the alteration of the landscape through both disaster and the reconstruction process that follows. The discussion brings out some of the ways in which documentary as a form makes the orientation of the social around the physical world more conscious. Quoting Henri Lefebvre's *Production of Space*, which overlays representational spaces over spaces of practice, Walker explores the effects created by interviews filmed in the locations that are the subject of the film, arguing that 'situated testimony realizes the materiality of testimony in the power of place' (2010: 85).

In the films discussed, the places are to some extent constructed. In *Wismut* three locations – Johanngeorgenstadt, Bad-Schlema-Alberoda and Ronneburg in Thuringen are brought together through railway and bus connections and the concept of the Wismut company itself, which isolated its activities and restricted its workers to the zone under its control. In Colorado, the mines in the mountains, the former site of Uravan, the communities of Naturita and Nucla, the proposed site for the mill Piñon Ridge in Western Montrose County, Telluride and the Cañon City, Cotter Corporation Uranium Mill are brought together by car journeys along the dramatic highways. In this way each film constructs the physical basis of industry as both the geology of the region and the infrastructure of the state.

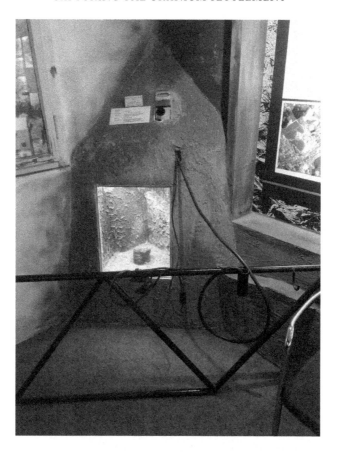

FIGURE 1.4: The Activist Clubhouse in Bad Schlema, museum of uranium mining. Visitors can take the Geiger counter from the stand front right and bring it closer to the ore behind the glass. The dial at the top shows the radioactivity level and the speaker amplifies its sound. Photograph © Helen Hughes.

In both films the issue is also not about places compromised by the disaster. The debate is about decisions made in the process of reconstruction. A social ecological reading of such spaces suggests a means to explore the potential role of witnesses who remain and embody a continuous investment of the landscape with memory and hence with meaning. The right to stay raises both social and ecological questions particularly when the presence of communities in particular places has been economically enabled for a national purpose that is no longer extant. What should the rights of citizens be in such cases? And what happens if there is no place for citizens to move on to? Just as Walker questions the nostalgia of the film *The Day the Levees Broke* and the wisdom of fighting to return to 'petrified topography' in Louisiana, Beraza's film interrogates the desire of young families to take risks to remain in this landscape.

Both films mediate the past through engagement with the community's current issues. They are involved with the 'continuing presence' of history (Assmann 2007: 13–14) but this engagement with testimony, storytelling, old songs, explanations, equipment, defunct identity cards, dusty photographs and 8-mm cine films is made relevant for the film by the persistence of the radioactive rock and its decay products that extend the presence of the mining industry into the future. The presence of the past in the *Wismut* tunnels and buildings is rendered uncanny in the film by the odd situation in which a political and economic system has been completely changed in a very few years. What is striking about *Uranium Drive-In*, on the other hand, is the absence of such an architecture leading to the initiative to restore one publically visible relic at least. While a museum in Bad Schlema displays a Geiger counter like the one in Koepp's film and allows visitors to point it at a rock in a glass container, Naturita has its signpost to the old cinema restored if not the venue itself.

NOTES

1. Cold War Patriots: 'a membership organization providing recognition and resources to the nuclear weapons and uranium worker community by connecting them with the benefits they have earned, including monetary compensation and free health benefits. We serve as the nation's leading voice in advocating for worker benefits, and as a resource providing one-to-one assistance for our members' personal questions' (Cold War Patriots 2020).

2. An important site for the production of fuel for nuclear bombs and energy was Grand Junction in Colorado, which became the centre of the Manhattan project's efforts to acquire uranium. Union Carbide was the company secretly contracted to carry out analysis and to produce enriched uranium. On the atomic heritage website there is a video of a recorded interview with J. P. Moore who worked as a chemist for the US Vanadium Company and then as Chief Chemist at Grand Junction, where he analysed uranium (Moore 2013). The video derives from the *Voices of the Manhattan Project* which the Atomic Heritage Foundation carried out together with the Los Alamos Historical Society. Moore was working in Uravan at the time he was transferred.

3. The rocks outside the mine are considerably less radioactive than the 'quality ore' found in the Wismut box. In that case the measurement was shown in röntgen, a European scale that measured the amount of radiation in the air rather than the absorbed dose. Using an online converter this comes out as 350.8 microsieverts per hour. As the permitted dose for the general public per year is 1000 microsieverts it would be a good idea not to spend three hours sitting on or very near these rocks – or indeed 116 hours sitting on the slag heap filmed in *Uranium Drive-In*.

2

Framing radioactive sites of evacuation: Nikolaus Geyrhalter's *Pripyat* (1999, Austria, Ukraine) and Toshi Fujiwara's *Mujin Chitai* (*No Man's Zone*, 2011, Japan)

Introduction

The two films discussed in this chapter both engage in observational shooting, capturing two locations and two communities experiencing radiological disaster in a particular place and at a particular time. As the accidents at Chernobyl and Fukushima have been broadcast across the globe, their documentary accounts are not motivated by information alone. Their entry into an evacuated area contaminated with radioactive particles is provoked instead by a perception of additional media and communications needs. In the case of Nikolaus Geyrhalter's *Pripyat*, a joint meeting in Vienna in 1996 of the United Nations International Atomic Energy Agency and the OECD Nuclear Energy Agency to reassess the accident at Chernobyl and its health and environmental effects after ten years provides the context for the camera to film the area. In the case of Joshi Fujiwara's *No Man's Zone*, which was shot in the Fukushima prefecture in 2011 shortly after the earthquake on 11 March, the context for filming is the imminent closure of the area around the stricken Daiichi nuclear reactor. Fujiwara was prompted to take a camera to the area in response to media reporting, which, in its focus on disaster, he felt was failing to capture what the people were actually losing in this moment.

In this chapter then the act of looking through the camera is doubled in the way suggested in the introduction by the radioactive environment. The image is lent a degree of self-consciousness by the history of the landscape and the orientation of the people to it. The films use a Cold War aesthetic of conscious observation in a reflexive response to the nuclear accident as an internationally mediated event. The camera is not a self-critical presence but in both cases the filmmakers use it as a means to access different kinds of behaviour in response to radioactive contamination.

Their portraits of individual lives and social history provide a counterpoint to journalism and to the generalizing statistical approach of the accident and radiological reports that referred to typically Soviet or Japanese behaviour. Precisely because they are contingent, in that they arrive in some sense arbitrarily at this time and place, the films allow for the possibility of diversity and individualism in their situated interviews and their approach to conveying subjective information about the accidents and the official response to them.

A specific context for the film *Pripyat* can be found in the OECD report which suggested controversially that the damage to health caused by the accident was perhaps less widespread and less severe than expected. At the same it reported that:

> An important effect of the accident, which has a bearing on health, is the appearance of a widespread status of psychological stress in the populations affected. The severity of this phenomenon, which is mostly observed in the contaminated regions of the former Soviet Union, appears to reflect the public fears about the unknowns of radiation and its effects, as well as its mistrust towards public authorities and official experts, and is certainly made worse by the disruption of the social networks and traditional ways of life provoked by the accident and its long-term consequences.
>
> (OECD Nuclear Energy Agency 1995: n.pag.)

Shortly after the meeting that produced the report, the Austrian filmmaker, Nikolaus Geyrhalter, in collaboration with the Committee for Chernobyl Questions of the Parliament of Ukraine, was given access to the exclusion zone to produce the documentary film *Pripyat* (1999). His assistant and unit production manager, who is audible as a translator and interviewer on the film was Ivette Löcker, and Wolfgang Widerhofer, a long-time collaborator with Geyrhalter, was responsible for the editing and dramaturgical shape of the film. The 30-km 'zone of alienation' around the site of the Chernobyl accident that had taken place in April 1986 had by that point already provided a setting for all kinds of stories looking back on the Cold War divisions of the twentieth century and on the painful process of change in the years leading up to and after the collapse of the Soviet Union. *Pripyat* offered a different approach in the form of an observational documentary that simply filmed the landscapes directly and collected witness accounts from people working and living in the zone.

In the case of Joshi Fujiwara's *No Man's Zone*, which was shot in the Fukushima prefecture in 2011 shortly after the earthquake on 11th March, the context for filming is provided retrospectively by a report commissioned by the Japanese government after the film was made. An independent international commission was formed to report on the nuclear accident at the Fukushima Daiichi power station, the first such intervention in Japan's history, and it concluded that the nuclear catastrophe was 'profoundly manmade' as in Chernobyl but, also as in the Soviet Union, attributable to the local culture, that is to the national development of the country as a whole:

What must be admitted – very painfully – is that this was a disaster 'Made in Japan'.

Its fundamental causes are to be found in the ingrained conventions of Japanese culture: our reflexive obedience; our reluctance to question authority; our devotion to 'sticking with the program'; our groupism; and our insularity.

(The National Diet of Japan Fukushima Nuclear Accident
Independent Investigation Commission 2012)

In a little volume called *Fukushima Mon Amour*, re-establishing a literary relationship between Japan, France and disaster via the echo between its title and *Hiroshima Mon Amour*, and containing essays that read like the voice-overs to essay films, Daniel de Roulet writes about his experiences as a writer in Japan where he is told 'the Japanese don't like to have foreigners talk to them about their history'. He asserts in an email to a friend in Tokyo at the time of the triple disaster, 'And now, doesn't your misfortune really concern us, despite what you might say? Aren't those employees at the Fukushima plant acting as kamikaze, atomic samurai? Heroism on a par with that of the workers at Chernobyl, who received such high doses that they had to be buried in lead coffins where they will continue to cool down for one hundred years to come' (de Roulet 2011: 10). The new consciousness after Fukushima, read through the new consciousness after Chernobyl, appears in this little book as a continuation of a global thought about despair in modernity and a call to revolt against government and industry.

The efforts of the different official organizations to understand the accident and to restore confidence in the industry through embedding it in international networks has been met with scepticism on the part of nuclear protestors. Sabu Khoso, in the book mentioned above, puts it quite clearly, understanding that a new international nuclear regime is being formed to contain the disaster and sustain nuclear energy: 'It is clear that this sector of global capitalism has no intention of abolishing nuclear power, and rather, is seeking to re-organize the technology, to manage it, namely to manage nuclear disaster, forcing people to get used to varied forms and degrees of radiation' (Khoso 2011: 49).

Responses such as these raise questions about the possibilities for observational cinema in establishing a context for communication in the aftermath of the reports. To what extent do the films reinforce what has already been said? Is it possible that they contribute in a different way to the reflexive process? Analysis of the films shows that they do support ideas expressed in official reports about the mental and physical effects of the accidents on the population. In addition, however, their capacity as social documentaries to focus in on the human condition itself as part of the way in which individuals reason about an event offers something that the official report cannot factor into a statistic. In the context of radioactive contamination, the observational documentary thus communicates something about common humanity that is not part of an instrumental process.

The invitation to film Pripyat

Pripyat, Nikolaus Geyrhalter's film about the decaying city and its river, was shot ten years after the accident. Geyrhalter was by this point experienced as a filmmaker in capturing landscapes scarred by warfare. His film *Das Jahr nach Dayton* (*The Year After Dayton*, 1997) followed a diverse group of participants in Bosnia. The shooting of *Pripyat* took place as the result of an agreement that gave him and his crew the opportunity to enter the restricted zone created around the accident to film the landscapes and to interview the people living and working there. The footage he shot would be made available to the European Commission and the ministries in Belarussia, Russia and Ukraine. Joana Rafael described the agreement as following 'the lives of those evicted from the kingdom of the well to remain in – living or commuting to – an apparently functional wasteland, enclosed by a complex architecture of exclusion and saturated in lethal levels of radioactivity' (Rafael 2009).

As Rafael points out, however, the film is not an exercise in anti-nuclear argumentation. It presents a series of montaged landscape sequences in the exclusion zone together with a number of portraits of people living and working in it. It is tempting to see it as looking in the spirit of many observational documentaries for the everyday life beyond the image of disaster, as an effort to normalize the extraordinarily named 'zone of alienation'. The Austrian Film Commission's explanation for Geyrhalter's film describes it in a rather cryptic way as 'additional information about events already widely known and presented to the public, and as a record of exemplary chapters of contemporary history observed from another point of view' (Austrian Film Commission 1999) raising the question as to what this alternative view point might be and how the documentary camera achieves such a thing.

Geyrhalter's frequently expressed journalistic-like intention to capture history on film through the portrayal of individual lives is played out in exemplary fashion. The decision to film in black and white already creates a consciousness of documentary convention in which black and white signifies the gritty and the real. By using black and white Geyrhalter managed to separate the film from the sepia and faded colour aesthetic of Andrei Tarkovsky's *Stalker* – strongly associated with Chernobyl – while still maintaining a connection with Cold War cinema. The film begins with a shot that comes directly from the cinéma vérité tradition. First a landscape, an establishing shot, and then the ruined cinema of the city, a self-reflexive sequence that draws attention to the medium and at the same time references the history of urban and rural landscapes that predate the moving image. The crumbling cinema signifies a putative end to this kind of image making in the post-nuclear landscape, but these decaying walls are for the film crew what the ruined churches and abbeys of the sixteenth century were to the Gothic writers of the eighteenth, a landscape for lessons in overcoming fear.

Measuring the zone of alienation

Pripyat frames the question of the nuclear age after Chernobyl in a similar way to the prose and image work in *The Chernobyl Herbarium* produced by Michael Marder and Anaïs Tondeur (Marder and Tondeur 2016); both works bring together art photography and scientific measurement. While Tondeur focuses on the plants on the ground in the zone, labelling her 'rayograms' (a form of photography based on Man Ray's photograms) with a quantity measuring the radiation level at 1.7 microsieverts per hour, Marder imagines the connections between the place and a seaside resort far away where he was as a six-year-old at the time of the explosions. In his texts Marder follows the spread of contamination across the world via the meteorological maps that show the radionuclides being carried over long distances across Europe. The documentary remains in and around the zone but it too explores the new sense of space, measurement and embodiment created by the consciousness of the radionuclides. The narrative moves from *Pripyat* the town, named after the river, to the periphery fences and gates, and then through into Chernobyl via the reactors and turbine halls that are still operating, and back out to the river, named, according to the local people interviewed, for its five tributaries. The search for meaning on this journey within the zone of alienation is structured by its institutional maintenance and the human stories of the people involved in it. The gaps in the measurements between the concept and the reality of the zone as a place of scientific exactitude offer an approach to the new phase of nuclear consciousness.

Now that Chernobyl has become a concept and a style that is closely overlaid with the history of documentary representations, it is difficult to retrace the ways in which *Pripyat*, shot ten years after the explosion, brought a new more precise image to the myth. There is an obvious affinity between the crumbling technocratic landscapes imagined by Tarkovsky and the exclusion zone around Chernobyl. It is the quantum crumbling vision of the Space Age that was the reply to the shiny surfaces of Stanley Kubrick's *2001: A Space Odyssey*, or to the electromagnetic force fields of the monsters in Japanese imaginary worlds. Digital post-production has now also contributed to the image of the place and the dramatization of the events leading up to and beyond the accident in the miniseries *Chernobyl* (Renck 2019). Now that Chernobyl itself has been declared a tourist destination and it is possible to visit the control room depicted in the series, if only for five minutes, the style and look of the era has become one of its meanings.

In black and white, the documentary sobriety of *Pripyat* works against the imaginative dramatization of the landscape, reinforced by long still takes. At the same time, the observational impulse is to record, as discussed in the introduction, the visible effects of radioactivity on the landscape, while drawing attention to its invisibility. The camera movements through the space set up a visual inquiry that hesitates, as in *Wismut*, between representing the environment as 'fatal' and showing its institutionally controlled version. The social interactions – the testimony and the documentation of the zone as a workspace – demonstrate to the crew and to the spectator the ways in which the people, all experts in this space, live in the new post-conscious world, in a measured rather than apocalyptic aesthetic.

Cinematography of black and white and symmetry

A number of aesthetic decisions made by Geyrhalter and his collaborators push the film on from its documentary or actuality role towards offering a study of the human condition after Chernobyl and after the Cold War. The use of black-and-white film stock emphasizes the film as oriented towards memory, turning its actuality footage into images that are not merely instantly past themselves but about the past before they are present. The opening shot to the film, before the image of the aforementioned crumbling cinema, is a static image of the city of Pripyat taken from afar. Its composition with small trees in the foreground and a dramatic cloudscape above the horizon suggests the timeless quality of an eighteenth-century landscape. The soundscape of birdsong and quiet machinery that accompanies the image lends the power station at the centre with its chimneys circled with paint stripes a cathedral-like quality. But the text that follows, explaining that this image is of a city in the middle of an exclusion zone, rescues the film back into its central role, which is to record contemporary life there at the end of the twentieth century, beginning with the exploration of the term *zone* as a measured and marked space.

> Pripyat was once the city where workers at the Chernobyl nuclear power station lived. Before the accident its population was 48,000 people. Pripyat is situated in the middle of the 30 km exclusion zone around the power station.

Pripyat is also the name of the river which flows through the zone contaminated with radioactive fallout. Today the area is a heavily guarded and still not fully evacuated exclusion zone.

In his last book *Camera Lucida* Roland Barthes made a distinction for photography between its capacity to provide historical information – the '*studium*', which here educates the viewer about the city and what has happened to it – and the '*punctum*', an elusive subjectively defined aspect of a particular image that catches the eye and draws out an affective response. Barthes explains the *punctum* in different ways, attempting to capture an irreducibly subjective phenomenon that is difficult to share but that is defined through Barthes search for his mother in photographs of her after her death. In the photograph, Barthes writes: 'There is a superimposition here: of reality and the past. And since this constraint exists only for photography, we must consider it by reduction, as the very essence of photography. What I intentionalize in a photograph is neither art nor communication, it is reference which is the founding order of photography' (Barthes 1982: 76–77).

Throughout the film *Pripyat* the camera tends towards the frozen quality of a still photograph even though in many of the landscapes it is not advised to stay for too long. The landscape is only once signified as radioactive by the sound of the Geiger counter checking a lorry as it leaves the zone. There is no music, no point note, to act as a guide to affect, as all the sound is ambient and related to the landscape itself. The insistence on the literalness of image and sound takes the film to the brink of total dependence on the contrast between the historical significance of the place set out by the opening titles and the undramatic patience of the framing, which gives the participants time to perform their work routines, to display their knowledge relating to their work and to recount their memories. One aesthetic choice, however, lifts the film as a whole and in individual scenes away from the documentary or the *studium* into the possibility of meaning besides this important function. There is an insistence throughout on symmetry within the frame so that positioning, even when it is not central, is registered as meaningful.

Situated memory and the 'punctum'

An important figure for the film who remembers the evacuation is Sinayda Ivanova Krasnozhon who works in a laboratory at Radek where she is part of the workforce carrying out environmental research on the exclusion zone. Krasnozhon herself embodies the difficulty for the evacuated population in bringing together her own expert understanding of the physics of radioactivity with her memories of the accident. She explains that her work involves primary research in gamma spectroscopy and that she analyses the presence of Americium, Strontium and Plutonium in materials such as foodstuffs, rainfall, soil or air brought to her laboratory. Her scientific role for all the years she has lived there also means that her measurements began before the region was contaminated by the accident. The fact that she has worked in the area since 1980 means that her participation in the film relates to more than questions about the radioactivity of the zone.

Questions designed to prompt the telling of Krasnozhon's own story elicit instead her expert opinion on the use of young soldiers as 'liquidators' during the crisis. She expresses her views sitting in the ruins of the sports stadium – where perhaps ideally for the film she would recount her experiences on the day of the evacuation. While she begins to argue that many people sent to Pripyat – filled with the Soviet enthusiasm for helping out in a disaster – were contaminated because they did not understand radioactivity and did not know how to behave to avoid the dangers, the image shows the disintegrating stadium as the historical realization of the story she is telling. Her unfinished or unresolved issues with the tragedy of the liquidators are superimposed on the image that shows young trees below where a running track might have been, where healthy and physically trained bodies might have run, so that her own body and the sports stadium with all its memories of physical achievements provide a referent for the sense of tragic loss. 'All those sent to help should have been experts', she says, 'but they were young lads who had no idea what you should do and what you should not do. They sat on the ground, drank water, went around half naked during that highly radioactive period. They had no idea' (Geyrhalter 1999). As Krasnozhon speaks, her voice and her animated face looking back and up to the camera repeat certain gestures and the word 'naked' covers both her performance and her memory of the susceptible bodies of the liquidators. The ionizing radiation is not visible to be seen in this image as a *punctum* but it is still the referent of vulnerability that the presence of the camera in the zone implies.

Although she explains that she has stopped visiting her old flat because her friends told her she took a long time to recover from the experience, she returns with the camera crew, taking them swiftly along the overgrown paths, while recounting her memories of walking to work after dropping her daughter off at school. The anger and sadness of her speech confirms the official reports about the population as a whole, in that she herself states that she has suffered more psychologically than physically. Her descriptions convey remarkably lucidly how a memory of a place may remain deliberately frozen while the reality has changed.

The distinction between the *studium* as education about the world and the *punctum* as the emotion attached to the idea that something has existed helps to understand the structure of the film which takes the viewer on a journey of understanding that begins with the irradiated zone as the location of a terrible accident

FIGURE 2.1: Sinayda Ivanova Krasnozhon relates her experience of the days after the accident at Chernobyl, Nicolaus Geyrhalter (dir.), *Pripyat*, 1999. Austria, Ukraine. Nikolaus Geyrhalter Filmproduction, firstchoicefilms, Österreichischer Rundfunk, Österreichisches Filminstitut.

and moves towards the quasi-presence of the image as the *punctum* or expression of an emotion that lives with the zone in its new sense of being. In its gathering of articulate individuals, the film represents the idea that decay and the observation of decay is not a temporary condition but a state of being that has already begun its own life along with the participants in the aftermath.

The safety officer's speech

All of the participants in the film have a role in observing or guarding the process of radioactive decay. Two, in particular, express reflexively the politics of the zone at the end of the millennium: the safety officer working at the nuclear power station, which up to 2000 was producing energy for Ukraine, and an elderly couple who decide to return to the zone after having been evacuated. It is worth thinking about these three people and their encounters for the way in which they represent human social life reorganized by the accident for the long term, their precise awareness of their surroundings acting as a model for the future.

When *Pripyat* was first shown, the fact that the power station was still operating was a surprise to many. The images that are in a constant effort to gain and regain symmetry again mirror reality in an unexpected way as the interior regime includes the normal safety checks of an operating nuclear power station to maintain an environment clear of radioactive particles while the exterior represents an irredeemably contaminated environment. The safety officer Nikolai Nikolayevich Suvorov leads the crew down the corridors to the wall that joins the third to the fourth block past the memorial for Valery Ilyich Khodemchuk who was working in the pump station at the time of the explosion. As they encounter the shift working in the control room, the safety officer explains 'This is a TV crew, don't be shocked, it's not the press. A TV crew just a film'. The alternations between following shots and portraits as Suvorov marches ahead down long corridors guiding the camera to the control room, the common room, the reactor space and the canteen mark off this section of the film as a harried counterpoint to the calm of the world outside. It covers the historically significant locations with explanations for the different parts of the control room, the reactor control section and the two sections dedicated to the turbines.

The social condition in Ukraine represented by the position of the safety officer who takes the camera crew onto the reactor floor and explains the machinery to replace the fuel elements is part of the route to understanding the new situation in 1999. In the canteen he explains that he gets good food for free as he works in a dangerous job, but he has not been paid his wages. The question about whether the reactor is safe puts the controller in a visibly difficult position. His assertion that he is engaged in making sure that an accident does not happen suffers from a lack of context and sounds as empty as all pure assertions about the safety of dangerous technology. The easier question about the sense of responsibility shines a light on the significance of the camera to him as the obligatory connection to the international community:

> Psychologically, morally, a great responsibility, to society, to my family, to my country, to the whole world. Yes it is a great weight, a very big responsibility. We feel it like that, especially when we get so much attention such as with this camera [broad smile at the camera].

Outside the power station the posters reinforce the aporia represented by the working nuclear power station at Chernobyl in 1998: *Workers of the exclusion zone! Let us protect Ukraine from radioactive contamination! Clean vehicles guarantee the prevention of the spread of radio-nuclides outside the exclusion zone! Keeping to the rules guarding against nuclear contamination in homes is key to a healthy life!*

All the participants in the film are asked to verbalize what they understand by the word 'zone'. Krasnozhon, for example, says it is a word she cannot use to describe Pripyat because in her mind it is still the place she knew from before. She explains that the word zone signifies the death and danger that she and her colleagues protect themselves from and it is still difficult to bring it together with her happy memories of her former home and workplace. A military guard at a road stop leading into the zone and an attendant guarding a store of radioactive vehicles confirm her definition of the zone as a dangerous and threatening place.

46

From their contributions it becomes clear that movement of materials out of the zone is a major issue as well as the monitoring of the time people spend in the zone. One of the vehicle attendants, in particular, appears afraid and uncertain about the radiation he himself is being exposed to, reciting the rules about the relative dangers of alpha, beta, gamma radiation, but mentioning that he thinks he will pay in future for having worked there. The vehicles awaiting the creation of a storage site include items that became famous through media coverage of the process of getting the plant under control, such as the helicopters from which various materials were thrown onto the stricken reactor. As they walk past the vehicles, the film crew are advised not to tarry. The film ensures in its coverage of safety maintenance that the image of the power station and the zone is correct. It is no investigative sting. But it cannot help but reflexively emphasize the hazardous nature of the landscape and the objects in it.

Living in the zone

Interwoven into the institutional structures guarding and maintaining the zone, the film represents a different portrait of it as a paradoxically natural, almost primeval place to live through the participation of Olga Grigoryevna Rudchenko and Andrei Antonovic Rudchenko. Their story is that they were resettled in the Crimea but decided to return in 1993. They also discuss the use of the term *zone*:

Olga Rudchenko: We don't call it 'the zone', we don't use the word 'zone'.

Andrei Rudchenko: What is the zone? The zone is what has been measured as the most dangerous place for radioactivity. A 30 km zone has been surrounded with a fence of barbed wire. We live in this zone, you see.

Olga Rudchenko: In the radioactive part.

Andrei Rudchenko: But look over there beyond the 30 km. What is over there? Does the barbed wire hold off the radiation? [laughter] So where does the radiation stop?

Several sequences that follow the Rudchenkos as they go about their daily lives imply that they might be reckless, the opposite to radiophobic. In an image that hints at a portrait of the couple as miraculous, Andrei Rudchenko is shown fishing in the river Pripyat. The camera is placed in the middle of the boat so that Rudchenko's rowing can be closely observed as he takes his fishing nets into the Pripyat river on his wooden boat downplaying the comment that the nuclear power station is only 12 km away. The sequences build up the reasoning behind the Rudchenkos' return in stages, focusing on the human need to retain a connection with place and between the past and present. Their testimony is coloured by the revelation that Andrei's job at the power station ended three days before the explosion so that he did not suffer the same fate as his friends and co-workers who died. The couple understand this as a miracle and live in their home as a testimony to their initial and long-term survival. They explain they are happy to contribute to knowledge by living in the zone voluntarily, mentioning that it was estimated that people would survive only seven years while they have been living there for twelve. They mourn the fact that their daughter, who was two months pregnant at the time of the explosion was advised to have an abortion and argue that people could have stayed because it was not actually known what damage would be done and people could have lived their lives and found out more about the real risk. They argue, in particular, that radioactive material could have been gathered together and cleaned.

The film interweaves the story of the Rudchenkos in its cumulative progression towards a synthesis of these various perspectives on the new kind of world. Gradually a revived, verdant and yet contaminated form of nature becomes an environment with an increased presence of wildlife for humans who have both it and themselves under constant surveillance. A long passage shot from a position that is characteristic for Geyrhalter's documentaries locates the new consciousness in a pictorial space between the eighteenth century and the twenty-first. Andrei Rudchenko drives his horse and cart along a narrow road. Rudchenko's awareness goes one step further than Sinayda Ivanova Krasnozhon's in acknowledging the threat posed by radioactive contamination but making a decision to balance it against other measures. The boat across the river is not an image of death and the horse and cart are not about returning to a state of unconscious dependence on the land with the competence of experts as an invisible distant background. Instead all the images relating to the Rudchenko's rural idyll are about a consciousness of the necessity of living with the radioactive environment. Subsistence farming and the technocracy of constant measurements come right up against each other.

Interviewer: Are you afraid of radiation?
Rudchenko: No. I can't feel any radiation.
Interviewer: Is the food irradiated?
Rudchenko: The food is safe
Interviewer: How do you know?
Rudchenko: It is monitored.
Interviewer: By whom?

FIGURE 2.2: Scientists come to take measurements of the water, while the Rudchenkos collect it for their household use, Nikolaus Geyrhalter (dir.), *Pripyat*, 1999. Austria, Ukraine. Nikolaus Geyrhalter Filmproduction, firstchoicefilms, Österreichischer Rundfunk, Österreichisches Filminstitut.

Rudchenko: People come from the laboratory and take the food we grow with them. And it seems everything is fine. We grow good potatoes, they are clean. We slaughter pigs, we have good bacon, clean bacon. Everything. We also hunt. We have everything we need. Grains, potatoes, everything is clean.

By the end of the film the present is portrayed as a network of people concerned with the cumulative monitoring of the land. The film does not present a utopia as there is a gap between the gathering of data and its application to everyday life. A scene with a woman in Poleskoje, just outside the zone, brings in a complaint about a lack of services and about resettlement, pointing to the problems created by depopulation. Filmed consultations between a doctor and her elderly patients demonstrate the ironic lack of current information to help her help them. The presence of a church, the priest spreading incense during the ritual of the mass, demonstrates that the scientific world lacks a sense of community that the people need to sustain them through the crisis. The film ends by showing a contrast. Two scientists set up a study of the river water with a fiddly piece of equipment while the Rudchenkos collect it with their traditional bucket carrying pole. Although they are all part of a social and environmental experiment, the community as a whole is not bound together by a shared understanding or belief about the world. The last conversation between the couple is about the way the plants have grown up and the animals have increased, particularly the wolves and the wild ducks.

Fukushima and speaking beside the triple disaster

In the discussion of the self-reflexive documentary in Chapter 1, Trin T. Minh-ha's way of speaking 'nearby' her participants is mentioned as a strategy to undermine the colonizing history of ethnographic filmmaking. Toshi Fujiwara's *No Man's Zone* is similarly subversive: an extraordinarily calm film, shot a month after the initial 9.1 magnitude earthquake off the northeast coast of Japan set off the 'triple disaster' on 11th March 2011, and which engages in various strategies to counter the effects of extensive international news coverage. Toshi Fujiwara and Takanobu Kato, documentary filmmakers, decided to shoot in the region in response to the images being broadcast by television. The relationship between moving image documentation and nuclear disaster had become an extraordinary phenomenon as CCTV, mobile phones, amateur filmmakers as well as the news reporters who happened to be in the region captured images of the earthquake and the tsunami that hit the coast half an hour later. It was a primary matter of concern that the nuclear power stations on the coast of Tōhoku had shut down during the earthquake according to their design specifications. At the Fukushima Daiichi Power Station the three nuclear reactors in operation at the time had shut down, but the emergency cooling system, powered by diesel turbine engines, had been flooded and caused both a blackout and the cooling system to fail. An evacuation of the region around the plant was ordered late in the evening on the day of the earthquake. Cameras trained on the plants outside the evacuation zone picked up the first hydrogen explosion in unit 1 which was broadcast in news reports around the world on 12th March. A second much larger explosion in unit 3 was also recorded and broadcast worldwide on 14 March. As the disaster unfolded and efforts were being made to rescue and then evacuate the population in the Fukushima prefecture in Tōhoku, the broadcast media were fully present.

There were few filmmakers in Japan with better training to tackle the ethical questions confronting the filming of the disaster. Takanobu Kato, who was the cameraman for *No Man's Zone*, had worked with Shinsuke Ogawa, the documentary director, who spent many years in the Yamagata prefecture in the Tōhoku region living with and filming the farming community there. Toshi Fujiwara, who directed the film, had worked with Noriaki Tsuchimoto, director of the series of documentary films about Minimata, a town in Japan whose community had suffered the terrible effects of mercury poisoning after the chemical company Chisso dumped its waste water into the sea where the community fished for food. Ogawa and Tsuchimoto were filmmakers who worked to gain a level of depth and integrity in their films in order to combat prejudice. Tsuchimoto, in particular, had investigated the case of the Minimata victims down to the last detail and demonstrated the terrible economic and social forces that had led to their suffering. At the same time he managed to uphold the dignity of his participants in his documentary that created a public platform for their struggle.

No Man's Zone is not an investigative film, nor is it a long-term observational film as it was shot over only ten days. In some ways it shares the qualities of Shevchenko's *Chernobyl: A Chronicle of Difficult Weeks* and *The Toxin of Chernobyl*, in that it is shot very soon after the explosions and shows some of the efforts being made to contain the situation. It is not, however, an officially sanctioned film, but rather an independent documentary with its own agenda. It does not engage with the response to the accident in the power station or interview the people dealing with it directly. Like *Pripyat* it is a film that offers an alternative approach to the representation of the disaster through engagement with the people affected. In her study of the film, Rachel Dinitto analyses *No Man's Zone* as a film that is concerned with 'memory, spectatorship, proximity and community'. She argues that it uses the images of debris to do the cultural work of creating a 'narrative of trauma' (Dinitto 2014: 341). Her point is that trauma narratives constructed by the community in the aftermath of the accident, including writers and filmmakers, focus on loss, responsibility and consequences in order to counter the strategy of TEPCO, the company that was responsible for the running of the reactor and so for the accident, in its efforts to move away from the accident to recovery. She notes that traditional stereotypes relating to Japanese culture that encourage citizens to repress their anger and engage in stoical acceptance were rejected in favour of an emphasis on unrecoverable loss and rage so that Fujiwara's film 'does not offer any comfort for those who view the images of debris or any hope for the residents that they will be able to return one day' (Dinitto 2014: 360).

There is much in the film that supports the reading of it as in solidarity with the strategies of such nuanced anti-nuclear protest. The commentary begins by directing its comments towards Tokyo: 'The nuclear power station existed in this region for forty years. For forty years Tokyo, four hundred and fifty kilometres away, has benefited from the electricity generated here. Nobody has really foreseen or has been prepared for a possible disaster to take place and nobody in Tokyo seems to know how to deal with it now'. The present is characterized by two kinds of landscape, both radioactive: low lying land next to the coast devastated by the Tsunami, and the higher verdant landscape around a village named Iitate 40 kilometres northwest of Fukushima, hit by the earthquake and contaminated by the radioactive plume. In the course of the film, as it portrays the encounters with different people in the region, the commentary expresses a concern that they are not angry enough and a gap is opened up between the response of the local people to the disaster and the point of view of the commentary. It seems as though the literal meaning of the landscape, its indifference to human life, its refusal to display properly its nature, overwhelms the effort of the commentary to draw any meaning out of it: 'in the end everything we have seen seems to have lost meaning when facing images of disasters that we cannot see. When meaning is lost we tend to start doing stupid desperate things but not these people'.

Local accident in a global context

No Man's Zone is a Japanese French co-production between Aliocha Films based in Tokyo and Denis Friedman Productions based in Paris. Almost explicitly the film explores what can be done with ten days location shooting in Fukushima, in Hamadori and in the Iitaté village, and a voice-over commentary. In an effort to move the film away from a focus on Japan alone and to connect the disaster with world events, Toshi Fujiwara explained his decision to work with the Lebanese actress Arsinée Khanjian to do the voice-over in English was an attempt to find a voice with an accent that could not be located in a particular place. This aspect of the film shows the gap between shooting and post-production. In an interview, Fujiwara explained his decision to film was because the television images, in their focus on horror, had failed to show what it was that people in that region had actually lost. His justification for collecting yet more footage was to create a coherently edited documentary which showed the beauty of the region that had suffered the disaster, and allowed participants time to speak about what life used to be like before it was so radically changed (Fujiwara 2011a). Thus at the end of the film when an intertitle dedicates it to 'all evacuees, refugees and survivors of the world, in certitude that one day they will find again their lives' there is a productive disjuncture between the achievement of its local focus and the international context in which it was finished and distributed.

Looking back at the film now across some years, its focus on what was lost does rescue it from the threat of emptiness by offering an absorbing local history of the region and of the generation that managed to survive there from the 1920s bringing up children and grandchildren all the way through to the triple disaster. It is a story moreover that forms a conspicuous sense of perspective out of the close proximity of death coupled with the pressure put on the time for narration by the radioactive environment and the process of evacuation. Near the opening of the film, as if by accident, the camera rises from the debris to show the seashore, stripped of objects, and captures in the distance the movement of bodies in white protective suits. The voice-over identifies these 'ghosts' as the police of the prefecture who themselves have come to look for bodies 'who might have been their neighbours from the same countryside'. The police are concerned by the prospect of their image appearing in the film because of the pain it might cause to people waiting for their relatives to be found. Burial is an important theme in the film. The participants discuss how it has not been possible to continue with the custom of the collective preparation of burials. The last thing that one of the participants, Yoshitomo Shigihara, does is to attend for the last time to his family grave.

In contrast with the stillness of the camera in *Pripyat*, *No Man's Zone* starts with pans, and hand-held shots of the port of Ukedo showing the chimneys of the Fukushima Daiichi Nuclear Power Station just beyond a forest. The voice-over commentary identifies the time as 41 days after the tsunami, the cause of the extensive damage that can be seen, making it the 6th April, some days before the region was declared an exclusion zone on 20th April. Because the disaster is so recent that the area has not yet been searched, the commentary explains that the cameraman is hesitant about the hand-held shot: 'he is worried he might be walking on the bones of the dead'. The moment is one of historic crisis and as in *Pripyat* it prompts participants to compare it with their experiences of World War II, particularly the reconstruction of the country in its aftermath. Their voices are heard in a context in which the elderly were most vulnerable to the effects of the tsunami and who were then also most affected when the creation of the exclusion zone and nightfall prevented the search for people trapped and injured. A study into the distribution of deaths that numbered 15,770 found that over half were people over 65 (Nakahara and Ichikawa 2013). The story that is being told is then that of the people who have been killed in the disaster.

Led by the participants, who are also in the end representative of those who guided the process of the official inquiry, the editing of the witness accounts draws

FIGURE 2.3: In the distance, framed by the debris, a camera operator approaches the police who are searching the area, Toshi Fujiwara (dir.), *No Man's Zone* (*Mujin Chitai*), 2011. Japan, France. Aliocha Films, Denis Friedman Productions.

the images towards a meaningful narrative, working back from the shock of the tsunami. The memories are elicited mainly in group discussions, which at first are relayed by disembodied voices while the image shows a view out of the back of a vehicle of the zone creating the sensation of moving backwards through space and by implication time. At first the voices are talking about the tsunami and the logistics of escaping it in Ukedo, including the efforts of people to go from the hills around down to the port to help those still trapped after the water subsided. As they all know the topography, they are able to describe it in detail and agree on what happened where. After a title appears on-screen indicating that it is three months later, the speakers become visible in their temporary housing outside the zone. The film allows their account of survival to unfold, told from a greater distance from the location where the events happened.

Japan and the great acceleration

As the film progresses the narrative reaches further into the past so that the history of the triple disaster turns into the kind of story that is now understood by environmental historians as a period called the great acceleration. In films the story is normally associated with the cities such as Tokyo, and the rural areas are portrayed as tranquil places where grandparents live, but *No Man's Zone* narrates how these regions too were part of growth and prosperity where people who remained with farming tended to do so as a hobby rather than as a main source of income. And so the worries about the position of the emergency generators before the accident are mentioned, along with the failure to report for fear of losing a contract. The story of how a military airfield became a salt field and then was sold to developers to build the nuclear plants is told. Accompanying this account of the changes in land ownership is another about the corresponding opportunities for work, from a day's work for 1.7 litres of rice, to double pay for road building connected with the nuclear power plant. Fukushima farmers who were working in Tokyo outside the agricultural work season could earn equally high wages closer to home from 1965 during construction works on the first plant at Fukushima. 'Thanks to the power plant I could get married and raise three children. I could give them decent educations thanks to the nuclear plant. Now we retired but our kids continue to work there'.

In a move from the parents' generation to the grandparents, another conversation offers a picture of a region that was agricultural before the development of the power station, with self-sufficiency farming, growing rice and vegetables and raising animals. This takes the narrative to a time before the great acceleration, offering a longer perspective. Towards the end of the film an elderly woman shows her garden that she has been growing for 60 years, commenting on the demise of even part-time farming in the area. As she shows off her wisterias and points out a field where they used to grow tobacco, the rice fields and the pasture for the cattle she explains they gave up farming years ago as her son earns a salary and works full time. Her perspective of the accident takes in her whole lifetime:

> We came here in 1941 when the war started. And the year the war ended we moved here in 1945. My father was instructor of growing silkworms. It was a time of food shortage, that's why he started farming. Our lives were never easy. Then suddenly this. We also survived the war, but that's life. We survived the war. We used to raise and milk cows. My husband worked in factories, also did seasonal labours, that's how we lived. Now I am eighty and suddenly I had to leave here, but that's life.

A 95-year-old woman who has been in the region over a period of 70 years speaks of her memories of starting to farm the uncultivated land, and making charcoal on the mountain to heat the home. When the filmmaker suggests that she can come back when she is 100 they all laugh heartily. The story is even taken back further than living memory through the encounters with many shrines in the landscape. A reference at the end of the film to the Japanese Buddhist teacher Kūkai touches on the social mores through the centuries, the connections between religion and hierarchy, between scholarship and engineering. As one participant says: 'We Japanese won't start a riot, we are educated and civilized. Just give us the facts'.

Evacuation as reorganization

There is no greater evidence for the ways in which the nuclear industries have reorganized social life than full-scale evacuation. In *No Man's Zone* this is counterbalanced by the story of how the organization of the social world around the nuclear power station was slowly built in the course of the Cold War. The turn to local people to create the narrative about what happened to them was an insight that took time to develop in the aftermath of the accident at Chernobyl. In the case of the Fukushima disaster it became a significant part of the official process of inquiry. Landscapes that tend to become frozen under the weight of the idea of radioactive contamination are reanimated through this perspective, which is both expressive of the trauma and suggestive of longer time frames and ways to work through it. The film frame, editing, music and commentary are all tools attempting to deal with the moment when the images of disaster threaten to become meaningless. Neither film turns, as do other films such as *Nuclear Nation*, to protest as a way to reshape the narrative. Instead each in its way is embedded in a specific place and cultural moment acknowledging the impact of customs and attitudes on the history of events.

The strategy of these two films does draw attention, however, to the need for some thought about the relationship between national identity and nuclear culture. Turning back to the quotation from *Fukushima Mon Amour* cited at the beginning of this chapter, sceptical about the effort to 're-organize the technology, to manage it, namely to manage nuclear disaster, forcing people to get used to varied forms and degrees of radiation' (Khoso 2011: 49), it is worth asking what the effect of the international networks created for the control of nuclear power in the aftermath of Chernobyl and Fukushima might be. It would of course be criminal for the international organizations involved in the control of nuclear energy not to be intervening energetically and compulsorily in local organizations, but the implication is that for nuclear power to continue to be produced, local culture also needs to be erased. But does such globalization also mean that local culture is to be rejected and condemned for being too heroic and communitarian or too hierarchical? Is the value system necessitated by the safe development of nuclear power acceptable? How might local diversity as well as the resilience of situated communities be protected in the face of the global view?

3

Placing the nuclear storage site: Michael Madsen's *Into Eternity* (2010, Denmark) and Peter Galison and Rob Moss's *Containment* (2015, USA)

Introduction

The problem of how to deal with the industrial waste produced by nuclear reactors is, as Ele Carpenter has argued, an issue that has brought the nature of the nuclear, or *nuclearity* more fully into the public sphere (Carpenter 2016). It is a subject that is difficult to debate without causing anxiety (Hora and von Winterfeldt 1997; Trauth et al. 1993), but it is nevertheless necessary to mark sites in order to keep people safe. In her discussions about the ways in which artists have been working with nuclear authorities to make sites more visible to more people for longer, Carpenter has pointed out the need for interdisciplinary, responsible, ethical and democratic systems of communication. She has also highlighted the qualities of art historical practices that have developed institutions to preserve and display artefacts over long periods of time, presenting art as an alternative to religious models such as a 'priesthood' or folk models. Carpenter frames the problem facing the artist as engaging with a phenomenon that on the one hand is not immediately apparent to the senses and on the other involves large expanses of time. What kind of aesthetic practices can deal with these issues?

This question itself has a remarkable history that is referred to in both *Into Eternity* and *Containment*, the two documentary films that are the subject of this chapter. In 1979 the US Federal Government approved the creation of an experimental site for storing the radioactive waste produced by its military programme to which it gave the name Waste Isolation Pilot Plant (WIPP). As it was clear that the plant would need to keep the waste isolated into a far distant future which could not be predicted, part of the process involved the appointment of experts to form an opinion on the kind of future societies that would be likely to inhabit the land above and around the nuclear waste repository in the next ten thousand years. An outcome of the futures project was the realization that future human societies posed a threat to the isolation of the plant and would be likely either by accident or by design to penetrate it. After consideration of the future societies, a panel of experts was brought together to design a marking system to deter those people from attempting to enter the site. The levels of information indicated in the quotation from the report set out the requirements for the markings to be prepared for the time when the waste depository would be permanently closed.

> Four levels of communicating about nuclear waste:
> Level I: Rudimentary Information: 'Something man-made is here'
> Level II: Cautionary Information: 'Something man-made is here and it is dangerous'
> Level III: Basic Information: Tells what, why, when, where, who, and how (in terms of information relay, not how the site was constructed)
> Level IV: Complex Information: Highly detailed, written records, tables, figures, graphs, maps, and diagrams.

> (Trauth et al. 1993: F-34)

Alongside the question of how to mark the waste debated by archaeologists, artists and communications scholars, nuclear scientists and engineers were designing systems to contain and store it. In the 1980s a model for processing and storing nuclear waste from power stations was developed in Sweden known as KBS-3. The Swedish word *kärnbränslesäkerhet*, meaning nuclear fuel safety, refers to a process for classifying and then dealing with nuclear waste over time. The process developed in Sweden has developed into an international norm and informs the temporary storage of nuclear waste worldwide. The model that deals with high-level nuclear waste produced by nuclear weapons programmes, and spent fuel from energy production, envisages storage in deep geological repositories created in rock that has not changed for billions of years. Finland is the country in which the world's first such high-level spent nuclear fuel repository is being created. The ongoing project, led by a company Posiva Ov in Finland, is called Onkalo.

Onkalo as a project is represented in the documentary film *Into Eternity* (2010) directed by the Danish conceptual artist Michael Madsen who interviewed a number of experts at the company using some of the concepts developed by the future societies project in the United States. The film thus brings together a contemporary engineering megaproject with a famous communications research project. Peter Galison and Rob Moss's *Containment* (2015) is also about nuclear waste disposal, this time focusing on the Waste Isolation Pilot Plant

(WIPP) in the United States itself, which has been relocated and delayed several times. The latest hurdle in the acceptance of its current location as a repository for high-level nuclear waste is the requirement to demonstrate it is safe for not ten thousand, not a hundred thousand, but for a million years.

For both of these films the subject of nuclear waste disposal itself is only one part of the problem of representation. As films they are tackling the more major issue of presenting a theme that is met with great hostility. In order to address developments in public policy regarding communication about nuclear decommissioning, it is not only the experts who must be involved in debate. Despite the fact that imparting the information about nuclear waste itself causes anxiety, laws about the location of it require informed consent (Trauth et al. 1993; Hora and von Winterfeldt 1997). Thus the question for the films is not whether they can add anything to a long established debate but rather whether they can present the issues in such a way as to meet current needs.

The idea that at least a section of the social world might need to be explicitly organized around nuclear waste products for such a large timespan appears to have reached the limits of reflexive modernity. How can any institution be created that would respond in a rational way to such a task? Nevertheless, as Kota Takeuchi, one of the artists working on the nuclear archive has put it, the actual problem for now is not how to communicate with the far distant future but just from one generation to the next (Carpenter 2016: 112).

The two films discussed in this chapter are projects that have responded to the task of representing the practical and conceptual problems in different ways. An analysis focused on their use of documentary as a genre brings out attempts to develop its capacity to respond to challenges of this intractable kind. They both demonstrate that risk communication is still a significant problem for industrial modernity. *Into Eternity* engages primarily with a contemporary expert community engaged in the development of technological solutions to the storage of waste in which they are assisted by public communications officers. *Containment* focuses on politics and public relations and attempts to communicate with local communities. In both cases the solution – the creation of the deep geological repository – characteristically shows up as itself an additional burden on the environment created by the industry. In the case of Onkalo the images of the tunnelling required to create the repository adds to the visualization of the reorganization of the world through uranium bringing it into the sphere of what is now called the Anthropocene – the shifting of rock itself a marker for the ways in which the human species has changed the planet. In the case of the WIPP, the natural site selected is not only contentious in terms of the ownership of the land. The adequacy of the expert opinion is also at issue. The documentary genre is stretched to the limits of its capacity to communicate.

Two activist films

Before discussing these two films that hold onto the possibility of democratic consensus, it is worth describing two activist films that engage with the subject in more agonistic way: the French-German television channel Arte's *Waste: The Nuclear Nightmare* (2009) directed by Eric Guéret, and the Swiss film *Journey to the Safest Place on Earth* (2013) directed by Edgar Hagen have set out the debate from an oppositional point of view. *Waste* responds to the lack of trust in the industry by looking into what happens to nuclear waste in different parts of the world, including the historical dumping of nuclear waste in the sea, and the military waste held in Hanford in the United States and in Mayak in the Russian Federation of States. The problems with the reprocessing plant in La Hague in France are discussed as well as the trade between France and Russia involving the reprocessing and storage of depleted uranium. The editing and voice-over commentary is relentlessly oppositional with workers involved in medical monitoring and in the nuclear industries in general portrayed as dishonest and evasive. *Waste* provides excellent audiovisual explanations, however, for how waste is produced, how it contaminates land and waterways and the various ways in which it is stored. At the end of the film it begins to move away from the statement of the 'nightmare' problem to set out the latest solution – the deep geological repository – which is being investigated in France in Bure in Meuse, a laboratory located deep underground. At this point the direction of thought moves from ascertaining a past in which the public has been 'systematically misled' to assessing the prospects for the future and the question of whether it is best to preserve or erase the memory of the site. The PR officer Martin addresses the question about how the site will be kept safe from future archaeologists, which, he says, is the 'poetic aspect', the 'science fiction' around this project. 'I'll meet you in 100,000 years to know. In any case memory and trust remain major issues'. The question is whether to trust 'man' or to trust 'geology' to keep the waste safe (Guéret 2009).

Journey to the Safest Place on Earth replaces this argumentative approach with an ironic account of the development of the idea of the deep geological repository itself. *Mise en scène* is deployed to undermine its main protagonist, Charles McCombie, who is shown preparing to be interviewed symmetrically placed on a Regency heart-shaped sofa with baroque wall panelling behind him. Before he speaks, the image is followed by another one in which the Cherenkov effect is used to indicate the high radioactivity of spent fuel stored in fuel ponds. The hypnotic deep blue emanating from the spent fuel as it is placed in position in the pool runs through the film as a symbol for the fascination with nuclear energy displayed by McCombie. 'The whole world has a big problem, and Charles McCombie has an unshakeable faith', begins the commentary accompanied by music that might accompany the opening to a comedic thriller.

McCombie was not the first to suggest the idea of the deep geological repository as the chronology provided by the website to the film indicates (W-Film Distribution 2013). His research was a response to the Flowers Report published in the United Kingdom, which stated: 'There should be no commitment to a large programme of nuclear fission power until it has been demonstrated beyond reasonable doubt that a method exists to ensure the safe containment of longlived, highly radioactive waste for the indefinite future' (Flowers 1976). McCombie's solution after five years research was published as *Projekt Gewähr* (Project Defence) and established a basis for continuing to build nuclear power stations even though no actual place had yet been located. *The Journey to the Safest Place on Earth* is an ironic title for an account of the difficulties in finding a site that is both geologically appropriate and has the support of the local community. Filmed in the different locations where experiments into ongoing geological waste repositories are being carried out, the film project throws up all kinds of situations that demonstrate the highly delicate nature of the project. The portrayal of an investigation with the name PANGEA based on undisclosed investigations by British Nuclear Fuels into sites in Australia is particularly painful. The film ends with an interview that takes place during a journey by camel in the Gobi desert in China where a local resident expresses his doubts. Water has been a theme throughout, representing the principal problem for containing the radioactive nuclides in the repository. As water is drawn up from a well for the camels to drink and the camels urinate copiously, the film makes its point clear.

Nuclear waste pitched as a concept film

To consider *Into Eternity* a promotional film would not be accurate. It is documentary funded by many different sources, not by Posiva, but produced with the cooperation of the company, which allowed access to the tunnels, to its workers, and to experts involved in managing the project. Because in the case of the treatment of the subject the future is represented as having already been addressed, however, it shares some of the characteristics of a promotional film. The construction of a discussion about whether and how to mark the site – the poetic aspect of the debate as it is called in *Waste* – serves as a way to inform the public about the project rather than as a debate about whether it should be built, circumventing the question of consent. The history of nuclear energy appears in two ways: first briefly as the radioactive waste that has been accumulated: 'we already have enormous amounts of nuclear waste. If this waste spills out into nature it will cause death and destruction. Large areas will become uninhabitable for a long long time' (Madsen 2008); and second in the form of cultural signs – retro colours, shapes, music and sounds associated with the history of radioactivity as a theme.

A reflexive reading of *Into Eternity* is about understanding its contribution at the time it was produced and released at the end of the first decade of the twenty-first century. Documentary during this period was experimenting extensively with the 'blurred boundary', as Bill Nichols has described it (1994), between fiction and documentary, and with a new hybrid genre sometimes referred to as 'mockumentary' (Hight 2013). This strategy is not so much about the truth of what is shown in a documentary as about the development of a tone that is no longer focused on the sober facts but on their cultural significance for their audiences. In a study on the 'promotional heritage' of nuclear communication *Speak No Evil*, Louis Gwin pointed out the problem with expecting utility companies to communicate the risks created by their facilities to the relevant populations, a situation that meant the companies both selling and cautioning about the same product (Gwin 1990). *Into Eternity* steps into these issues through its focus on the sign or the 'marker' rather than the radioactive waste, embedding the direct representations of radioactivity that do appear into the film within the discourse of promotion and cultural significance rather than of argument or protest.

Thus the beginning of the film uses footage that shows a fuel rod being removed from its location in a reactor to a fuel pool where it will be stored until it is cool enough to be moved to a more permanent location. Bookmarked by an intertitle reading 'nuclear waste' in retro orange on a black background, the sequence reveals a highly automated and precisely controlled industrial process that contrasts starkly with the chaotic images of nuclear waste shown in protest films. The mechanical movement of the complex steel units taken along internal passages to their new location in clean water gleaming a purplish blue from the radioactivity is accompanied by music from the album *Radio-activity* by the German pop group Kraftwerk. Uwe Schütte has traced the progress of this album from its neutral beginnings inspired by electronic music broadcast on the radio to becoming part of overt anti-nuclear campaigning from the early 1980s (Schütte 2020: 76–87). *Into Eternity*, however, sticks with the version from 1974 that Schütte describes as 'ambivalent'. In the images, the engineers working on the fuel pools are shown in slow motion that signifies their work as precise because it involves risk. The image as a whole is cool drama rather than dirty secret.

In an interview, Madsen has explained his approach to finding ways to communicate with the scientists and engineers involved in building Onkalo, saying that the orientation towards the future 'was designed to relieve the scientists of the agenda of today and help them speak more freely' (Madsen 2011). With the focus being on the expert debate about what society and the earth might be like in 100,000 years, *Into Eternity* presents a clever strategy both acknowledging and setting aside the current environmental debate in order to shift attention to the ways in which new technologies have been developed out of the debates in the past.

In their history of the environmental effects of the great acceleration, McNeill and Engelke (2014) ask why the humanities focused during the Cold War period on the problem of knowledge and of the sign rather than on the material issues relating to the environment. An analysis of *Into Eternity* demonstrates how the focus on the 'marker' and the problem of communication it involves does, in fact, address a material problem. The lack of a fail-safe communications system able to inform and produce instant cooperation out of a mass society creates obvious difficulties for globalized hazardous industries. On the other hand, conceptualizing communications media as separate from the materiality of modernity allows them to escape the questions about their role in the creation of the present. An understanding of them as an integral part of reflexive modernity – as reflexive institutions – highlights the possibility that mass communication – or the assumption that such a thing is possible – is capable of creating new problems of its own. The debates about documentary truth highlighted during the Cold War might be conceptualized as acknowledgements of these issues, not only deconstructing the ways in which media worked traditionally, but also highlighting the ways in which they continually create, as Miriam Hansen put it, 'new modes of organizing vision and sensory perception, a new relationship with "things", different forms of mimetic experience and expression of affectivity, temporality, and reflexivity, a changing fabric of everyday life, sociability and leisure' (Hansen 1999: 60).

The marker project and *Into Eternity* set up a fiction of a direct conversation with human beings 100,000 years hence, following up on an earlier fantasy in which a team of linguists, anthropologists, architects and communications experts attempted to imagine a system of communication across time that could be maintained for 10,000 years. Nuclear energy in Finland actually has a relatively short history. Having built a research reactor in 1962 it constructed its first nuclear power plant in 1977 in a project that involved cooperation between the East and the West. Even this small amount of local history is excluded in the film *Into Eternity*, which instead draws on the Waste Isolation Pilot Plant marker project. The report, not named in the diegesis but clearly known by the expert participants, is transformed into a simplified thought experiment. Subtitled *A Film for the Future* the participants are asked to imagine they are speaking directly to people in a far distant future, thousands of years hence, warning them about what might happen if they intrude into a deep geological depository that has been created, filled with highly radioactive waste from nuclear power production, and sealed not to be disturbed again. It was a documentary experiment that met with a very positive response. Peter Bradshaw writing for the *Guardian*, a paper that specializes in environmental topics such as nuclear energy, responded with particular enthusiasm: 'why isn't every government, every philosopher, every theologian, everywhere in the world discussing Onkalo and its implications? I don't know, but they should see this film' (Bradshaw 2010).

The concept documentary, which sometimes tends towards the ambiguous tone of the mockumentary, participates in reorienting the attention paid to an issue in a different way to the self-reflexive film discussed in the introduction. It is a form that was beginning to be developed at the end of the Cold War and can be associated with some of the strategies used in *The Thin Blue Line*, a film about the search for legal truth by Errol Morris. As part of the film, Morris included film noir inserts, capturing an imagined forensic mind-set that distorted the evidence. In *Into Eternity* playful references to the physics of space and time are inserted but in this case to permit the absorption of information and messages about nuclear risk.

Cool expert documentary

Into Eternity, then, can be understood as participating in these experiments in representations of the long-term nuclear project. In its use of voices it draws on more recent media and the popularity of Scandinavian television, Scandinavian cool or Scandi-noir. Interviews with participants such as Timo Äikäs, with his thoughtful and hesitant soft tenor voice, labelled on-screen as Executive Vice President Engineering in Onkalo, his signature underwriting his statements, bring the thought experiment to the experts as they address the intruders: 'we want you to know that this is not a place for you to live in'. Peter Wickberg, Research Director, nuclear fuel and waste management, Sweden, is inserted as a confirming voice, extending Äikäs's account of the impossibility of getting rid of the waste by sending it into space or putting it into the deep ocean. Timo Säppälä, the senior manager in the communications department at Posiva, the company that has developed the waste disposal system, interviewed onsite, brings in a factual tone estimating the amount of waste in the world as between 200 and 300 thousand tonnes. Michael Madsen's own voice, with its soft mid pitch imagining the future, responds calmly but slightly eerily to the information that comes his way.

Within this context, contemporary anxiety about the uncontrollable nature of radioactive waste is stylized and so relativized. Madsen's comments express fear: 'we already have enormous amounts of nuclear waste. If this waste spills out into nature it will cause death and destruction. Large areas will become uninhabitable for a long long time'. Parody horror sequences, however, such as the hand-held

camera approach through the trees to the large white country house, location of
the interviews, undermine the seriousness of the tone. The pronounced silence
within which the voices slightly echo alternates with music and ambient sounds
associated with the thriller genre. In these ways the film allies itself with a mock
naïve position of vague fear about the future. The rational thought processes of
expertise do not come across as attempts to wish away the fear but to answer it
with practical even if incomplete solutions. The film does not take on the tone of
the World Nuclear Association, for example, which currently states, 'Safe methods for the final disposal of high-level radioactive waste are technically proven;
the international consensus is that geological disposal is the best option' (The
World Nuclear Association 2020). The idea of burying the waste is acknowledged
as imperfect and the central discussion about how and whether to label the site
maintains the popular impression of nuclear discourse as unduly and deceptively
sanguine.

After an extended take travelling with a lorry underground into the tunnel, the
first extended interview sequence is with Wendla Paile, who is the Chief Medical
Officer at the Radiation and Nuclear Energy Authority in Finland. The information she has to present concerns how harmful radiation is to life. The gravity of her
statements, like those of Madsen, are balanced with humour, as she is represented
as an almost ghostly Marie-Curie-like figure. She appears in a copper-coloured
room with an operating table placed under an arch holding medical instruments. A
man is teleported in a Mélièsian style onto the table, after which Paile also appears
wearing a pink teeshirt under her white coat. Just as she appears, an electronic
sound gathering like accelerating wind comes to a sudden stop. She points out
that radiation was discovered only three generations ago, and despite the playful effects, her straightforward words that explain radiation as 'a sort of energy
that can penetrate deep into your body' again confront the anxiety posed by the
invisible threat. As the body of the male patient is scanned she is shown moving
through the white shiny spaces of the building, sometimes hitching a ride on a
trolley, and her voice, now detached from her body, describes the symptoms of
radiation sickness. 'Never stay in an area with an enhanced radiation level', she
concludes, 'and never ever touch a strong, radiation source!'

The communications manager for the Onkalo project leads the section on
reasons for preferring deep geological storage to long-term cooling ponds on
the surface of the earth. The film does not rest, however, with the opinion of the
manager, turning to a Professor of Theology Carl Reinhold Bräkenhielm, of the
Swedish National Council for Nuclear Waste to say that all citizens 'irrespective
of whether they like nuclear power or not' need to deal with the problem of the
existing waste and not allow the problem to be covered up by arguments about
the future production of nuclear energy. His point, however, is not a response to

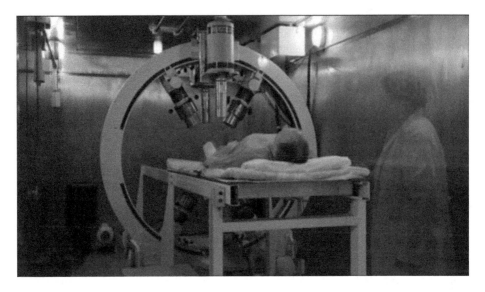

FIGURE 3.1: Wendla Paile, Chief Medical Officer at the Radiation and Nuclear Energy Authority in Finland, appears in the frame to explain radiation and its potential effects on the human body, Michael Madsen (dir.), *Into Eternity*, 2010. Denmark, Sweden, Finland, Italy. Atmo Media Network, Film I Väst, Global HDTV, Magic Hour Films, Mouka Filmi Oi, Yleisradio.

whether the Onkalo project is the right way forward. An insert in which Sami Savonrinne, a 'blaster' at Onkalo speaks about his experiences of time slowing down and speeding up in the tunnel where he works, leads to a less tightly controlled sequence in which different points of view about the future can be placed next to each other. The recording of the explosion in the tunnel on camera is a cinematic event in itself. Later in the film a sequence is inserted where several blasters working together insert tubes of Kemix explosive with Nonel detonators into holes they have drilled into the rock. They are shown as faded images in time lapse walking into the temporary buildings and into the tunnel.

These striking scenes accompanied by contemporary classical music by Philip Glass or Avo Pärt, which also works emotionally through patterning and repetition, communicate what was an optimistic period for nuclear energy at a time when the accident at Chernobyl was coming under control and the accident at Fukushima had not yet happened. The film communicates the message that chaos could break out on the surface of the earth but the deep geological repository would probably be able to isolate this particular nuclear threat. The extended debate about how to communicate with the future portrays social organization as inconsistent and vulnerable, making the obvious cost of this high tech project worth paying. The computer images of the geological space deep in the earth represent it as a new creation, not owned yet by anybody, a kind of emptiness. The engineers, non-speaking subjects engaged in working in the nuclear industry and in the tunnelling project, and represented in slow motion, are transient, as are we the spectators, but collectively part of the bigger enterprise of saving future generations from the disaster prepared by our forebears. None of this space is as yet radioactive, making it like a house that is about to be moved into, an ideal place for play.

Physics and the conceptual 'no-man's land'

Containment, directed by Rob Moss and Peter Galison, contrasts strongly with *Into Eternity* through its consistent focus on contaminated spaces where efforts to contain radioactivity have either failed or are on the brink of failure. This film-making team is unusual. Both are professors at the University of Harvard: Rob Moss is chair of the department of visual and environmental studies; Peter Galison is professor of the history of science and physics. Galison's first book, *How Experiments End* (1997a), asks a very precise question about the fuzzy process of bringing an experiment to a conclusion. The editing of the material gathered together in *Containment* relates to the thesis that it is the ending that defines scientific progress. In his books Galison has explored the history of science by focusing on relationships between agents within the scientific community. The drama of this history is found in a precise chronology of interactions between practical problems, theoretical and experimental physicists and publically funded grant giving bodies. His book on time, *Einstein's Clocks, Poincaré's Maps: Empires of Time*, looks at how the practical questions posed by the difficulty in synchronizing time across and between nations was the context for the wholesale shift in knowledge represented by Einstein's theory of relativity.

Galison's focus in his books, however, is on the moment just before the conceptual assumptions are upturned. He shares this with Moss who also has an abstract and ethically concerned approach to filmmaking. They are both interested in a kind of conceptual no man's land where old concepts are still understood and still provide the means of navigation but new concepts are also being validated and producing unexpected results. *Containment* is a film that explores or perhaps seeks to provoke such a moment in which it is acknowledged that there is a concrete problem. A fundamental conflict in perceptions about radioactive risk means that there is no location where nuclear waste products can be stored other than where they currently stand. The film maps out this moment by cycling three locations: Fukushima shortly after the accident in March 2012, the WIPP near Carlsbad New Mexico and the river flowing on the border between South Carolina and Georgia. Many scenes express intense anxiety about the ways in which the future is being determined by the present. The film is concerned with overcoming this emotion but it does not go beyond it, meaning that the film concludes with no ending.

While setting out the issue and its history *Containment* constructs an audience capable of imagining a different future world in which the nuclear waste crisis can be addressed. As such the film is a concerted attempt to use the culture of documentary cinema as a tool, in more traditional language, as a means to 'make a difference'. The 'difference', however, relates to the very process in which documentary cinema has been constructing the social world of the nuclear industries, acknowledging that it has played a role in creating the existing crisis.

The unusual nature of the film can be traced back to the circumstances of its making. Unlike the normal course of events for independent documentary, there is no specific occasion that prompted the making of the film. The films discussed so far in this book can be contextualized historically. *Wismut* was prompted by the reunification of Germany and the beginning of a remediation project. *Pripyat* is the result of new access to the zone of alienation around the nuclear disaster site in Chernobyl, and *No Man's Zone* of the imminent closure of access to the environs around the Fukushima accident. *Into Eternity* documents the building of the nuclear waste repository Onkalo. Other films are concerned with making a particular argument: *Pandora's Box* is concerned to make a pro-nuclear statement, and *Uranium Drive-In* to explain why local people are keen to re-start the nuclear industry in Naturita, Colorado. The film *Containment*, on the other hand, was initiated as part of a research project entitled 'Socio-technical aspects of nuclear waste and its long term storage', with the output of a feature-length documentary 'the scientific, political, and ethical issues adjacent to the problem of the socially responsible disposal of nuclear waste'. The Waste Isolation Pilot Plant east of Carlsbad in New Mexico is named as the central location for the film as 'the only fully-licensed, operating geological repository for nuclear waste in the world' (Galison 2013).

In the account of its approach the abstract refers to 'trading-zone studies', an anthropologically inspired concept developed by Galison in his book *Image and Logic* to describe how scientists and engineers managed to trade expertise in the development of radar and particle detectors. The important aspect of this approach is its recognition of subcultures in the world of science and technology that are not necessarily able to cooperate even when the issues are grave, as in the case of long-term nuclear waste disposal. The purpose of the film, then, is to depict 'collision as all sides struggle to shape a contested nuclear future'. The film, like other socially motivated films, has been used to reach a broader audience through contacts with outreach organizations. The core audience is still understood as policy makers and environmentalists but it is also concerned with 'groups and citizens traditionally not positioned to participate in science policy' (Galison and Moss 2016).

The documentary function

Although films are often used for outreach purposes, the specifics of how and whether they have an impact is highly contested. Pat Aufderheide listed all the reservations about measuring impact in an article on the Participant Index, an approach that quantified impact by asking audiences to score their response to a film in terms of the intensity of their engagement and the real-world changes in their behaviour, writing that:

> measurement clashed with the reality that film was an art form; that immediate post-facto measurement could not take account of serendipity; that highly targeted films could reach small audiences with enormous real-world effects; that all measurement was an example of neoliberal creep; that measurement subsumes a filmmaker's agenda to the funder's; and that measurement turned the filmmaker into a tool of activists.
>
> (Aufderheide 2016: 34)

The impact of *Containment* as a film is ongoing (with this written response being one piece of evidence). Its impact on audiences is not likely to be a change in behaviour but the more traditional environmental aim of a change in awareness. The awareness in question, however, is not only about the risks posed by nuclear waste but also the risks posed by failure to reach consensus. Galison has confirmed in interview that the goal for the film from early on was to replace the alternation between pro- and anti-nuclear positions with a statement 'in the world already, whether we like it or not, this is the legacy of more than half a century of nuclear weapons and power production. What are we going to do? It's an obligatory problem with no simple answer' (Galison and Moss 2016).

The utopian idea that a film should leave the viewer to think through the issues presented is not, of course, new. It is an optimistic characteristic of the political cinema of the United States and Europe during the Cold War. There are also several examples of contemporary cinema that largely exclude words and emphasize the aesthetic quality of the image in order to create space for contemplation (Hughes 2013). Some problems with this approach were identified very early by Bill Nichols in his article on 'The voice of documentary' in which he complained that filmmakers were failing to take responsibility for their films and allowing participants to hijack them (Nichols 1983). In the case of *Containment*, however, it is not a utopian idea but necessity that has left the film open ended. The more significant point, however, that solutions need decisions – a point put by the documentary *Waste: The Nuclear Nightmare* discussed above (Guéret 2009) – is deferred by the film, which, as Moss put it, is a 'film to engage in thinking not choosing' (Galison and Moss 2015).

Containment: *The film*

Containment is made up of sequences relating to three sites: the Fukushima Prefecture after the triple disaster, the Savannah River Nuclear Site and its environs, and the Waste Isolation Pilot Plant in New Mexico. These sequences are contextualized with interviews, other observational sequences, archive footage and animation all of which present the history of nuclear waste and its containment. Three stories are told. In Fukushima the story of the disaster could have been even worse if a fuel pool had also exploded. In the Savannah River Nuclear Site a legacy store from the Manhattan project during World War II has become an unmarked de facto nuclear waste recycling and storage facility. In New Mexico a community has accepted the Waste Isolation Pilot Plant as a high-level nuclear waste repository only for an accident with a package of waste to cause it to shut down for an extensive and expensive clean-up. This last story of the Waste Isolation Pilot Plant also includes discussions about the Markers project with some of the experts who were involved. Animations represent the markers as well as a children's story centred around a character called Nukey Nuke who transmits knowledge about the site across the generations. This story interacts with historical sites and childrens' stories in Fukushima that have handed down knowledge about the possibility of a tsunami across the generations.

Where is radioactivity to be found in these three narratives? The point is that it is dispersed. In Fukushima it has escaped via the plume containing radionuclides emitted from the nuclear reactor after the explosions. It leaks out from the Savannah River Nuclear Site. The WIPP, constructed to contain nuclear waste turns out to be flawed also, and the project to consider how to communicate with the far future about a nuclear waste repository appears to be a fantasy in assuming that there is a sealed site that could last so long. Radioactive contamination is, then, represented as distributed about the world in the way that protest documentaries have been portraying it since the 1970s.

In his *History of Documentary* Barnouw cited an NBC documentary broadcast in 1977 with the name *Danger! Radioactive Waste* as the first to deal with the waste problem. The hour-long programme covers many issues, including the use of tailings to build housing. It covers issues at the Hanford Site, where the first reactor to produce plutonium was built as part of the Manhattan project, and the last part of the programme shows the site of the Waste Isolation Pilot Plant near Carlsbad in New Mexico as it is being tested. The film is similar to *Containment* in its mix of concern and calm analysis. It points out the long timespans involved. It orients itself to the future. The commentary goes on: 'when you are talking about radioactive waste you are talking about the future, thousands of centuries from now' (Konner 1977). It measures the length of human life against that of the radioactive waste and uses wildlife to signify a non-human perspective. With an image of fox running around outside the site, a former worker employed to assess the safety of a proposed twenty-year plan comments: 'sooner or later these wastes are going to come back and bite the hand of the human race if it happens to be around at the time'. Exactly the same comments about it as a problem that is not going to go away are made. As a fish is taken out of a river and cut open, the voice-over commentary states: 'It is safe to assume that as the quantity of waste increases so too will the contamination of the environment. Perfect containment is not even considered a realistic possibility or goal. Some release of radioactivity is a certainty Americans must face' (Konner 1977).

Barnouw also mentions another film about the Savannah River Nuclear Site. Nominated for an Oscar in 1991, *Building Bombs* is described in the *New York Times* as 'an effective muckraking film because it doesn't scream hysterically' (Holden 1991). The film is actually more than this. Interviewed for the DVD edition, Susan J. Robinson is eloquent about the efforts of the first-time filmmakers to shift the emphasis in the film from the protestors to the former workers at the plant and the story of their crisis of conscience. The striking aspects of the site, besides its historic role in the building of the hydrogen bomb in the 1950s, are its size of around three hundred square miles, and the discovery that the turtles native to the region had become radioactive. The community as a whole, which, characteristically for nuclear sites, expanded from thirteen thousand to fifty-five thousand, is also cited as displaying an interesting ambivalence about the industry. 'Increasingly apprehensive employees had petitioned for a health-impact study, but the request was vetoed as unnecessary' (Barnouw 1993: 309). The shift from the protestors to the community captures the complexity of the history of the site and the story of a gradual shift in attitude towards it and towards Cold War history. According to Robinson this meant that they could begin to structure the film 'very consciously for people who weren't what we would call core environmentalists or anti-nuclear activists [...] regular people who are interested in understanding issues in our times and who have a desire to see good policy set and potentially speak up' (Robinson 2007). *Containment* updates this account, showing an ecologist some fifteen years later studying the radioactive turtles and alligators kept onsite and a scientist explaining the issues connected with storing high-level waste. A portrait of a local pastor on the other side of the river updates on the community and its sense of anxiety about the spread of contamination, pointing out the lack of markers highlighting the specifically radioactive hazards to local people.

During the Cold War, radioactivity had already been portrayed as leaking out of sites in the United States, the original context for the WIPP markers project that has become so internationally resonant. *Containment* takes a further step and, in the context of the accident at Fukushima, joins this restricted national debate to the international situation. It is a difficult move to make, which can only be fully understood as symptomatic of a long but hesitant process of coming to terms with the Manhattan project itself. Jerome Shapiro has written about the explosion of genre films with atomic themes after the invention of the atom bomb in the United States and its deployment at the end of World War II in Japan. He pinpoints 1958 as the high point of a wave of films crossing genres he labels atomic bomb cinema, which is 'not a genre like the western, but a unique category of films that crosses the boundaries of many genres' (Shapiro 2001: 12). Arguing strongly against Susan Sontag's dismissal of the films as a mark of the inadequate response to atomic warfare, Shapiro claims that the films used the 'ancient apocalyptic tradition of continuance' (Shapiro 2001: 10) to help their audiences to deal with guilt and the kind of total war or devastating accident the technology had unleashed.

The opening sequence to *Containment* can be understood as introducing something approaching an argument about an ancient tradition of continuance but it is quite a complex network of cuts that leads to such an interpretation. It emerges out of a process that is attempting to deal with a complex historical situation in a very abstract way. However it is seen, the film is concerned with finding a path towards consensus about what to do with nuclear waste, particularly legacy waste from World War II and the Manhattan project, but also waste produced by military operations during the Cold War and by civil energy production. There is an awareness that the kind of democratic public consensus required is a long way off. It requires evenly distributed prosperity, equal opportunities, universal high-level education, particularly including knowledge about radioactivity, internal reconciliation over the past contamination of indigenous land, and reconciliation over nuclear test sites in the pacific. Once all of this is achieved it may be possible to persuade the population as a whole to acknowledge the nuclear waste, take ownership of it and work out an agreed strategy.

In the meantime for *Containment* this aim has to be backgrounded while three sites are foregrounded: Fukushima in Japan, the WIPP in New Mexico and the Savannah River Nuclear Site facility, built in the 1950s displacing the local populations in South Carolina and Georgia. The WIPP is a key part of the foreground as, despite its unreality, it has first of all to be deconstructed as a fantasy of the late 1970s and early 1980s. An interview with Bob Forrest, former mayor of Carlsbad New Mexico, shows him declaring his belief in WIPP 'from the very beginning'. His vision is typical of an opportunistic attitude that trusts in belief itself and in salesmanship while cultivating an awareness of the wealth promised by the project. The problem of climate change is introduced in this context through another flat landscape with scattered nodding pumpjacks extracting oil while Forrest speaks about the reality of global warming and his belief that nuclear energy would help with the problem. He suggests that the problem for nuclear energy is merely the question of where to put the waste and declares that the problem is solved in the form of the WIPP near Carlsbad.

This portrait is attractive and encourages the thought that a bout of historical amnesia would simply solve the problem. The markers project associated with the WIPP, however, brings in the first catch. The ambivalence that has accompanied the nuclear industry from the start is expressed in a point comparing a similar project on communication with extra-terrestrials. While the capsules created to show human life to aliens present the best of us, the WIPP marker project presents to the future, our descendants, the worst of us: 'we were showing them something that perhaps we should be the least proud of. Our shortsightedness, our inability to always consider the consequences of our actions' (Galison and Moss 2015). The WIPP, the markers project, and *Containment* are all about considering consequences but they all come up against an awareness of the impossibility of seeing very far into the future. The obviously dated vision represented in the markers designed for the WIPP demonstrates the way in which the future also dates.

The discussion about the spent fuel pool crisis in Japan is the strongest argument put forward in the film for an urgent debate about nuclear waste management in the United States. Interviews with Yoichi Funabashi, Co-chair of the Fukushima Investigation, and Gregory Jaczko, Chair of the US Nuclear Regulatory Commission ((2009–12), narrate the circumstances of the nuclear meltdown before Naoto Kan, prime minister of Japan 2010–11 recounts his memories of the moment when he considered the possibility of the end of a whole state: 'If that worst case scenario had come to pass I feared that decades of upheaval would follow, and would mean the end of the State of Japan. We escaped by a paper thin margin'. In comparison with such a crisis, the release of trace amounts of plutonium and americium at the WIPP after an accident appears to be the least worst option. This implicit point is followed up in Allison McFarlane's statement about the impossibility of perfect containment: 'we're fallible' 'and there's no 100% guarantee with whatever we decide. There's no way to ensure whatever that we will be able to keep this material isolated from humans in the environment. There's no way to ensure that at all, no matter what you do. There's no way to make this stuff go away. There's no magic'.

The third site foregrounded in the film, Burke County Georgia bordering the Savannah River Nuclear Site facility, paradoxically brings in several calm green scenes even if there are warnings amidst the trees while Rev. Willie Tomlin talks about the narrow border between his county and the nuclear facility. These are complemented by scenes in Japan as two elderly men talk about their experiences of destruction in Tokyo during World War II, but state that the disaster in Fukushima is worse because they cannot go back and rebuild: 'For sixteen generations it was our home and my generation is going to be the last one. We'll have no home.

FIGURE 3.2: A warning is left for future inhabitants in Aneyoshi, Japan after a tsunami. Fumi-hiko Imamura comments that such warnings are not taken seriously, Peter Galison, Rob Moss (dirs), *Containment*, 2015. United States, Japan. Redacted Pictures.

That's hard to bear'. The cut back to the Savannah River Nuclear Site and the statement that 'the site has become a de facto high level waste storage facility' demonstrates a terrible symmetry in which the pastor's statement about his sparse community having no power and the handing down of the problem to later generations raises more unanswered questions about history and environmental justice.

In all then, the film presents an impossible foreground against an impossible background and there does not seem to be much hope of finding any solutions except in the sequences of cuts between these scenes that offer various possibilities related to the possibilities raised by the collision of communities. One cut indicates the ways in which debates going on within the industry in one part of the world can stand in for conversations not taking place elsewhere. An interview with Allison MacFarlane, former chair of the Nuclear Regulatory Commission, about the circumstances in which fuel pools in which high-level waste is stored become unsafe, is curtailed when she states that she is not permitted to talk about these circumstances. After this the film cuts to the WIPP and the question of how the site might be breached. The point here appears to be that the WIPP discussion is actually a proxy debate about the need to mark and contain the de facto long-term storage sites at every nuclear installation. 'If people start getting sick and don't know why, not marking it would be an immoral act' applies to the Savannah River Nuclear Site as much as to the WIPP. A further cut between the markers and the beautiful but contaminated landscapes in Fukushima complicates this further, implying that the debates about the waste markers are a fantasy because they are imagining the waste set aside and contained in a neat way. What actually exists are landscapes in remote places in several parts of the world that are contaminated. Paradoxically in Japan some examples of ancient warnings are found, showing the level to which a tsunami rose long ago together with advice not to inhabit the land below. This and the traditional story told in schools of man who saved his village by setting his hay on fire demonstrates the more pragmatic reality.

The deliberative intention

The film has been taken by its makers around many different institutions as part of the effort to promote a constructive and creative debate about nuclear waste. The filmmakers have spoken about the different responses in different countries around the world. Although they say they are 'drawn to problems where there isn't a solution' the idea seems to be that the film will increase the possibility of finding or agreeing to a partial one. In doing this the filmmakers are in tune with Brian Winston's critique of the expository documentaries of the British documentary movement that tended to present solutions rather than real problems (Winston 1995). Winston has updated this point in a later book calling for documentaries to focus on open current questions (Winston 2008). These discussions after the screenings support the film in its openness, but they also demonstrate that understanding the status of the images presents its own difficulties.

The need for the presence of filmmakers to bring documentary back to a more deliberative rather than the more internalized, contemplative, autonomous form is also part of a broader development that has been the subject of debate for contemporary documentarists looking to expand the form beyond character and storytelling. The recently founded online journal *World Records* hosts some of these debates such as the manifesto 'Beyond story: An online community-based manifesto' launched by Alexandra Juhasz and Alisa Lebow (Juhasz and Lebow, 2018). In a discussion published in the same volume, Charles Musser, the film historian has spoken about his research into the long history, or *histoire longue durée* of documentary film and his finding that the name documentary could be thought of as a temporary label, accidentally applied when there was no name for the successful films circulating such as *Nanook of the North* (1922). The word *documentary* has since then stood in for a form that, using intertitles, dispensed with the need for the accompanying lecturer making documentary viable as an autonomous form in the same spaces as the feature film (Glick and Musser 2018).

Musser goes on to say that documentary film should be understood as but one possible form, along with the lecture and the demonstration, that has developed ways of bringing together different kinds of evidence in support of the 'display of knowledge'. The idea of *Containment* as a deliberative documentary fits well into this account of the flow of different modes and forms that has characterized documentary history and that is discernible today in the rapid development of different frameworks in the online environment. If we put *Into Eternity* and *Containment* together they do appear to be variant forms relating to different spaces. *Eternity* works in the cinema as a standalone film, incorporating Madsen into the film itself as a figure addressing the audience from the screen. Its play with genre and associated affects mark it out as a thought-provoking and entertaining informative film. *Containment* as a film brings together different kinds of knowledge from different parts of the world in a way that invites questions to the accompanying crossover team of scientist and filmmaker. Coming from an institutional context, the film is incorporated into an ongoing research project that is part of a much bigger question about an uncertain future.

Not fitting into the mould of the activist film, the need for *Containment* to be accompanied returns it to this longer history. The accompanied film as document is able to address the future from a living present rather than the imagined one of the markers project, but it also creates new questions about an unaccustomed dynamic. How much information is needed to be added to make the message understood? Is the idea of decidability undermined by the explanations and expansions of the filmmakers? Pat Aufderheide's research into the relationship between documentary and impact ends with a discussion about what lies behind the polarized positions – between documentary as an art form and documentary as a vehicle for communication and social change. She puts forward the possibility that the role of the documentary filmmaker, which since *Nanook* (1922) has had a stable definition for nearly a hundred years, may be changing as a result of a more participatory culture. An alternative to this view is that the effects of greater participation in decision making are felt more and more in the form of documentary with none more acutely felt than in this question of the future of nuclear waste. As a form that has accompanied the history of modernity, its reflexive development is part and parcel of the relationship between individual awareness of the human condition and the creation of risk.

4

Remembering the architecture of nuclear power: Volker Sattel's *Unter Kontrolle* (*Under Control*, 2011, Germany) and Ivy Meeropol's *Indian Point* (2015, USA)

Introduction

The evacuation zone and the siting of high-level nuclear waste have been joined as documentary subjects by nuclear decommissioning projects. Historically, the industry has attempted to build the cost of decommissioning into the business plan for many commercial power stations, and the decommissioning of nuclear power stations represents an opportunity for technical services. The interest for documentary filmmaking varies from the explosive images of the demolition to the empty premises after the radioactive material has been removed. As decommissioning projects have accumulated, however, in the wake of Fukushima in particular, awareness of the passing of an era has grown, transforming the subject from mega engineering tasks to the examination of the culture of the nuclear industries.

In this chapter, two films will be discussed, which represent the disappearing spaces of nuclear power generation. Volker Sattel's *Under Control* is a film that is built on a visual appreciation of its qualities across many different sites all over Germany. Ivy Meeropol's *Indian Point* focuses on a single power station not far from New York City, viewing it from inside and outside as a landmark and focus for a generation. Both films are made in the context of imminent closure so that the timely record of the buildings and people that they offer is part of their raison d'être. The recording of a still intact industry as it considers the possibility of its own demise is the special circumstance that gives these films an even greater visual intensity, adding its aura to the invisible presence of radioactivity.

Documentary filmmaking has historically been associated with the disappearance of the premodern world, arriving as it did together with the forces that modernized and changed the cultures as they were being recorded. The preservation of premodern cultures on film is an archival reflex. To what extent is the recording of modern industry archival as well as reflexive and what kind of meanings are preserved? Is it possible to capture the ways in which the world of nuclear energy is organized beyond the buildings represented or does the Brechtian assertion that an office building says nothing of the organization it represents pertain here too? When it comes to nuclear power, an industry full of contested sites for landmark buildings, is the archival reflex about capturing their power or their ambivalence or the conditions of their demise? In what sense does the film feed into the future of the industry if there is one? How can the radioactive materials that are left behind be integrated into the story?

The study of these two films explores what their contribution is to understanding the present state of the nuclear industries, considering in particular the ways in which they represent for most power stations the first cycle of what is a very long site process of building, energy production and return to green field status. What emerges very strongly in the films is the relationship that is created between the industry, its architecture and a particular generation. This has already been noted in the case of *No Man's Zone* and the history of the post-war Japanese economy. As the finite nature of resources becomes more apparent, including the question of the extraction of uranium for the power stations, this matching of generations with prosperity becomes an important aspect of intergenerational justice. There is, nevertheless, a sense in which the films represent a move away from accusing the past to a search for evidence about why the past unfolded in the way it did.

A difficult film

In 2008, when Sattel was awarded a Gerd Ruge scholarship to realize his project *Under Control* the nuclear industry was a central topic of political debate in Germany. The press release about the award described the proposed film thus:

> Against the background of the current debate about the phase-out of nuclear energy, the graduate of the Film Academy Baden-Württemberg examines the history of a utopia in *Under Control* - and the legacy of a high risk high technology.
>
> (Filmstiftung NRW 2008)

The Gerd Ruge scholarship is a prestigious award given by the North Rhine Westphalia (NRW) Film and Media Foundation to young filmmakers as an opportunity to make an intellectually demanding documentary. After the award in August, the filmmaker has 18 months to develop a high-quality film for cinema distribution as well as television broadcast. The Kuratorium junger deutscher Film also supported the film along with the television channels WDR and ARTE. In 2008, the year that Sattel received the award, the nuclear industry in Germany was in the process of being phased out. In 2002 the Red-Green Coalition government (the Social Democrats [SPD] and the Green Party had won the 1998 elections) and, headed by Gerhard Schroeder, had reached a consensus with the energy companies and passed a new version of the *Atomgesetz* that represented an agreement between government and the major utilities to phase out nuclear energy production by 2022. Nuclear power stations in Germany would have a life of a maximum 32 years, meaning that as each plant reached that age it would be shut down. No new nuclear power stations would be built and existing generators would also produce only a limited amount of energy before closure.

The phase-out was highly contested. The major opposition party, at that time the CDU (Christian Democratic Union) headed by Angela Merkel, was strongly against the agreed time scales. One of CDU's policy pledges was the revocation of the *Atomgesetz*. In 2003 the Stade plant, a light water reactor on the river Elbe north of Hamburg went offline after 32 years of power production. Obrigheim, a pressurized water reactor on the Nekar some 40 km west of Heidelberg went offline in 2005 after 36 years. As part of a negotiated agreement the CDU/SPD (Social Democratic Party of Germany) coalition government of 2005 continued with the policy but when the CDU won the Federal elections in 2009, forming a coalition with the Free Democrats (FDP), the terms of the *Atomgesetz* were altered, extending the time that plants could operate before closure. Seven of the plants would operate for a further eight years on top of that agreed, and ten plants would continue for an additional fourteen years. The ban on building new power stations remained, however. The period in which Sattel was making his film was one in which the nuclear energy industry had experienced a stay of execution but the overall context was still a phasing out of the technology. All nuclear power generation even after the revision of the *Atomgesetz* was planned to cease by 2036.

Interviews with Volker Sattel when the film was premiered at the Berlin Film Festival in February 2011 reflect the heightened political debate about the delayed phase out of nuclear energy that took place between 2008 when the film production gained funding and 2011 when it was released. In an interview for *Spiegel Online*, an international magazine, Sattel expressed his views formed after a period of three years of research and production work on the film. Acknowledging that the majority of people in Germany were against nuclear power and that their efforts had forced the industry into safer procedures, he stated that the film was nevertheless 'an attempt to lift the fog and bring some clarity to the discussion, so we can talk about it more calmly' (Sattel 2011b). Reviewers of the film generally understood it as a requiem or an elegy for the industry, which Sattel confirmed, pointing out that the film begins with working reactors but goes on to those that have shut down, have failed to start, and to waste repositories. In the *Spiegel* interview he also refers to the future:

> We have some huge tasks ahead of us that cannot be underestimated. The dismantling of nuclear power plants here and elsewhere is a major exercise that will cost billions of euros. And obviously there is the problem of what to do with the waste. Our whole society must consider this properly so we can find the right solution. Even though the maximum is being done with regard to safety and security, there is always a risk. Finally though, with this topic, you end up concluding that neither one side, nor the other, is correct. It comes down to a need for careful assessment. It should not be a decision based on emotion.

The film *Under Control* is then about the end of an era but also in part about the need to maintain the same vigilance about safety as the industry developed its techniques for decommissioning, decontamination and high-level radioactive waste storage. The industry had been compelled to plan for this period from 1959 when the first *Atomgesetz* was formulated as a statute for the peaceful use of atomic energy and ionizing isotopes including measures for protection against the dangers they pose.

As has already been seen in the case of the uranium mining industries in the Erzgebirge, there has been a period of intense investment in Germany in decontamination and making safe since the end of the Cold War. *Under Control* can be understood as a continuation of a process of documentation and reflection in Germany that can be found in the films already discussed, such as Volker Koepp's *Die Wismut* of 1993 and Joachim Tschirner and Burghard Drachsel's *Die Wismut: terra incognita* of 2007 (and 2016). While these films focus on the uranium mines, Sattel's film concerns the institutions involved with nuclear power production, the power stations, the training facilities, the scientific research institutions, the international organizations and even a trade fair. Although the nuclear industry at every phase has been an experiment with a high public profile, moving images of its interiors and procedures is quite rare. The film thus offers a picture of the industry at a critical point in time, twenty-five years after the accident at the Chernobyl power plant, twenty years after the end of the Cold War and in 2011 twenty-five years before all nuclear power stations were due to close. It is a film about remembering *not* to forget, rather than 'remembering to forget' as Madsen put it in *Into Eternity*. The approach to memory has something Kierkegaardian about it, in the sense that repetition is understood as the remembering of the past on behalf of the future. *Under Control* could be said to exemplify the moment for such a philosophy, using the form of the documentary to reflect on the present as an archivable resource for the future. Sattel described his sense that the technology had in any case slowed down its own process of change through its own monumentality.

> It doesn't matter how many nuclear Renaissances there are in other countries, the technology won't last beyond the 21st century. The film is playing with a vision of a bygone future. With some shots I had the impression at the editing table that I had shot archive material. Many people look as though they are from the nineteen-seventies.
>
> (Sattel 2011a)

Archive and archaeology

All of this adds up to an understanding of the film as a descriptive project that found an audience in the aftermath of the accident at Fukushima. The subtitle to the film is, however, about an 'archaeology' rather than an archive of atomic energy, an indication of a desire to see the industry as not only historical but positively ancient in the present. The use of the word 'archaeology' can also be understood, however, as the development of a method within the documentary film of creating a boundary, a 'border of time' as the philosopher Michel Foucault put it in his 1969 work *The Archaeology of Knowledge* (2002: 147). Its shots of exteriors, interiors, of workers training and at work, of health and safety procedures, of inspectors, system maintenance, trade fairs, conferences and even critical observers, are all presented in the film as a kind of taxonomy of an industry that will soon be historical if it is not historical in spirit already. This vitrification of the industry, the creation of an elegy for it, can be seen as an attempt to recreate the 'positivity', to use Foucault's terminology again, which allowed an energy industry to be created out of nuclear fission despite the obvious risks, despite the reservations of many scientists, despite the economic cost and in the face of continuous citizen protest in the form of mass demonstrations, civil disobedience and legal action.

A Foucauldian understanding of *Under Control* as an archaeology of the nuclear industry as a practice is not, however, a straightforward proposition. In his essay in the volume *Foucault at the Movies*, helpfully titled 'Versions of the present', Patrice Manglier restricts his analysis to 'films that adopt a position in relation to the past and a critical relation to that past – films that have done what Foucault did in the field of history' (Foucault et al. 2018: 66). This strategy is wise because Foucault himself wrote explicitly that his method was designed to study historically distant discursive formations, explaining: 'it is not possible for us to describe our own archive, since it is from within these rules that we speak, since it is that which gives to us what we can say' (Foucault 2002: 147). It is part of Foucault's method to understand the past as difference, as discontinuous with the present and only discernible as such. The film cannot be 'archaeology' in Foucault's sense, then, because it is describing the present, albeit a putative or hoped-for ending to an aspect of that present.

Despite the subtitle then how is it best to approach the film *Under Control*? Might it, perhaps, be taken simply as a visual description of the industry made to preserve it for archaeological studies in future? It could be described as a kind of salvage ethnography, a recording of a modern culture, perhaps an example of the culture of the great acceleration that is coming to an end (McNeill and Matsumoto 2017). Sattel's film is distinctly different to Koepp's *Wismut* that engaged with the workers of the uranium mining company Wismut SDAG using architecture, objects and re-enactment to commemorate their past explicitly, allowing for critical reflection on the meaning of their history. There are very few moments of reflection in *Under Control*, giving each case a greater prominence. An interview about an hour and a quarter into the film with Armin Grunwald, physicist and philosopher and head of the Institute for Technology Assessment and Systems Analysis (ITAS) in Karlsruhe, summarizes the position of those working in the nuclear industry whose 'life energy and entire biographies were dedicated to this technology':

> In the 1960s people still thought that energy consumption would grow at the same rate as economic growth. They drew up graphs with sharply rising curves and planned enough power plants to cover those energy use projections. And they built way too many. And then, as atomic energy lost acceptance that led to the pleasant after effect that they could stop building plants but still had enough because they had built too many. Ideally we would be able to create technology that could continually be adapted to accommodate new developments. But that's impossible. See the nuclear power plant example. Once the plant's there, it's there.
>
> (Sattel 2011c)

Grunwald's analysis is placed in the film after a sequence that shows how the industry has been inscribed since 1957 in the street names – Maier-Leibnitz-Street, Heisenberg-Street and the Schrödingerweg, followed by Lise-Meitner-Weg leading to Max-Born-Weg – all around the first research reactor, the *Atomei* (Atomegg), which with its iconic egglike shape, has been preserved. The long tracking shot along a road of low housing and garages supports Grunwald's story of a technology that was developed to accompany the 'economic miracle', a period of rapid growth in West Germany in the 1950s and 1960s. The housing and the cars speak of improving life styles and growth in energy consumption. Just as the power stations were built so too were the new housing estates developed around them. After Grunwald is shown speaking on-screen, there is a cut to a boating club on the Rhine near the Phillipsburg power station. The power boats are moored along the banks with the cooling towers behind. A reflection of one of the towers in the water with clouds and blossom petals represents an entire lifestyle of concrete buildings and powered vehicles that has lasted for 30 years or more: 'why can't we stay here?' a child's voice pipes up as the family moves on from an aggregate site.

This sequence frames the entire film as a retrospective and hence it might be argued that it can no longer have the reflexive quality that would feed back into the development of the industry beyond a long-term aim to eventually look back and reflect. A major aspect excluded from the film, however, gives a clue as to the reflexive role that the film does in fact have. The film does not allow any anti-nuclear demonstrations between 2008 and 2010 to spoil the picture. Instead, in its structure the film analyses the spirit of the age as a paradoxical regression towards ever greater precautionary steps that in the end themselves characterize the aesthetics of the nuclear age. As such it is clear that the film is not intended as a critique but as a representation of an industry that is in any case in a complex process of closing down. The point that there is a need to preserve the skillset of the workers it represents only supports the idea that it was a dream that slowly decayed as the dangers and difficulties became ever more apparent, and that the closure of the industry will be as complex and as in need of skill as the rest of its history.

Visualizing radioactivity

The film starts and finishes with two sequences that represent radioactivity. At the start there is a minute of film showing images in a large cloud chamber at the

FIGURE 4.1: Cloud chamber images at the start of the film show the paths of particles emitted from a radioactive source, Volker Sattel (dir.), *Under Control* (*Unter Kontrolle*), 2011. Germany. Credofilm, Westdeutscher Rundfunk, ARTE.

Science Center Spectrum in Berlin. The trails left by alpha and beta particles can be seen as bright lines of light shooting in different directions as the credits begin. This is clearly not the same as the flashes of light created on the surface of the film stock by radiation at the site of the accident in Chernobyl but it does represent a way of seeing or tracing the path of radiation moving through the air. At the end of the film Franz Wagner, a scientist at the new research reactor at the Technical University in Munich (FRM II) is thanked for lighting the passage of final credits with gamma radiation, which produces on the film a varying green glow. The cuts from the cloud chamber through various shots up to the electricity pylon signals visual coherence as a strategy for the film: a slow tracking close-up of a fuel rod moves to a diagram of a control panel, to a reactor undergoing refuelling or maintenance, to an image of a steam turbine, the inside of a cooling tower with the water falling down into it, to an external shot showing the size of the tower and finally its connection to an electricity pylon. At the same time this sequence signals the shots as a way of looking that attempts to combine the technical with the social and the aesthetic. The camera is placed on the floor of the reactor as well as travelling high across the inside of the biological shield looking down on the workers below. External architectural shots of constructions containing nuclear reactors – domes and squares and the iconic shape of the *Atomei*, represent the development of commercial atomic energy as an aesthetic cultural moment as well as a sociopolitical one.

Readable images are thus presented by the team that worked together to create a coherent and attractive montage. The colourist Roland Murrer has created a tone that captures something of the grey-green of a nuclear technocracy. The research and script for the film were produced by Volker Sattel with Stefan Stefanescu who was also responsible for the calm interviews and the informative green MS DOS titles that punctuate the film. Thilo Schmidt assisted Sattel with the camera work while Tim Elzer and Nikolaus Woernle worked on the sound composition, a largely ambient sound track with several witty moments. The sound montage mixed by Ansgar Frerich reinforces the Sattel's editing assisted by Stephan Krumbiegel particularly in reinforcing the impression of a thinking camera engaged in the creation of a dramaturgy out of the industry, led by Stefanie Gaus. But, as might be expected of a film that was supported because of its aim to challenge audiences, they need some scrutiny to be deciphered. Despite the variations in the shapes of the power stations, some sporting domes, others more prosaically cuboid, their monumentality and their concrete finish, the arrangement of the buildings in clusters decorated by trees places them in a period between the 1950s and the 1980s. November 1982 (Nekarwestheim 2, completed in April 1989) was the latest date that construction began on a nuclear power station in Germany.

A sequence of nuclear sites

The sequence of nuclear installations follows up on the attempt at rigorous consistency noted in the connection between the cloud chamber and the electricity pylon with an equally meaningful path from the optimally working nuclear power station. The stages, including as they do the sites of significant accidents, power stations that never opened and half built edifices left abandoned, add up to a humanly and environmentally expensive record of trial and error both in a technical and a social sense. A point that comes across as powerfully reflexive is a kind of terrible balance between the forces pushing for the development of nuclear energy and those trying to suppress it. It is as though the traces of the industry constitute a record of the struggle between Beck's 'traditional' industry, working with the hierarchies of the late nineteenth- and early twentieth-century, and the reflexive modernity that he himself promoted.

A portrait of Grohnde Nuclear Power Station in Lower Saxony is, from the point of view of anti-nuclear protestors, perhaps the most provocatively neutral part of the film. It is a montage of external shots from varying distances and different angles showing the reactor dome, the cooling towers, the turbine halls and the electricity substation. The section also includes some commentary as part of the diegesis as a guide explains the siting of the power station as the outcome of the presence of a water supply in the river Weser, a large plot of land for sale by a local monastery and the willingness of the local community. This last point goes uncommented even though Grohnde has been the site of many large demonstrations from the planning stage to the present. The guide shows a working model and asserts that the plant is so up to date that engineers 'lick their lips' over it. The film does not only show the engineering of the nuclear power station itself but also the general office and its connectedness via computers and telephones to the rest of the plant.

As the film cuts from the office where an announcement is made to the space outside where the announcement is heard, the film takes on a slightly unreal, fictional quality. The codes used for the messages are left unexplained, a situation that is left in place as workers around a large table at a meeting make their reports. The images of people at work are then replaced with images of visitors being shown around the plant. The camera positions jump around from spectacular hall to small shed to tour group in the distance, to an explanation of a procedure to create a cloud over the power station to deter an attack from the air. As night draws in, the buildings are shown floodlit and the clouds billowing from the cooling towers tastefully obscure and reveal a bright almost full moon.

This opening to the film points to the attractions of the nuclear power station, its everyday mystery, but it also establishes the ways in which the camera is engaged in discovering the body of the power station through the focus on its parts.

In his essay 'What film is able to do' Dork Zabunyan notes Foucault's understanding of cinema as a form of knowledge as a process of 'stripping down' through which film creates an understanding of an institution. He understands Foucault's comments on film as indicating a 'search for a certain sobriety of images', which he also describes as a 'requirement for sparseness' and an 'art of poverty' (Foucault et al. 2018: 20). In *Under Control* Sattel restricts his filmmaking to what can be captured by the lens and by the sound recorder but he also stages small moments, such as a worker walking across a space to open a door. The restrictions imposed, such as the lack of explanation for what is discussed in the board room, divert attention away from the details of the day to the structure of the daily meeting and the awareness that the workforce is accustomed to these routines, to their calm orderliness. The portrait of Grohnde is important for the demonstration of an allegiance to the nuclear power station from the men suspended on the sides of the huge water towers to the men around the table (and one, possibly two women).

Once this ideal is established, however, the film moves into its portrait of the industry as one which has reflexively altered its practices continually over the years. The faintly fictional feel of the Grohnde presentation is followed up by a sequence at the Simulator Centre in Essen where a number of control rooms in power stations have been set up for training purposes. Such centres have existed since the 1970s and have developed progressively in response to accidents which have revealed weaknesses in the systems and also in human behaviour (IAEA 2004). The camera becomes overtly playful at the opening to this section and in a close-up on the 'reactor safety panel' follows the lines, arrows and ampersands. The language the tutor uses to explain procedure is remarkable for its chronic avoidance of negative vocabulary. He talks about heading towards an 'ungood situation' if the'good zone is left' then the 'little lamps light up'. The explanations for the training provided by the instructor are an important part of the film, particularly for the way it provides an explicit discussion of the relationship between people and technology. The precision of the talk is remarkable. The generalization that everyone makes mistakes is qualified by a quantization – ten mistakes per hour in the case of drivers: 'We have enough backups to lower the chance of complete failure', 'the chances are 1 in 10^{-7}' or 'in everyday language not humanly possible'.

At this point in the simulation the camera moves to one side and reveals a corridor while the participants continue to discuss. As procedure is explained the panels of wiring connecting the simulator panels come into view in a movement that is interpretable in different ways as snooping or as a way to avoid too much detail of the simulated situation being understood. However it is seen, it is the beginning of the descent that begins with a model built to create an understanding of two accidents that took place at Three Mile Island in 1979 and at Biblis Nuclear Power Station in 1980. Made of glass the movement of the water through the system can be observed along with the 'hammer' phenomenon that was identified as the cause of the accidents. For the film the symbolism of such transparency is obvious. The participants working in the simulator are confronted with this syndrome and we see how the system gradually responds, ending with sound and light alarm signals. The view of this scene from an observation room separated from it by glass puts the film into the territory of the fiction film *The China Syndrome* (1979) that came out shortly before the accident took place in Three Mile Island. After the participants have left, the camera again goes off to take a look at the details: the handwritten logs, the papers, books and charts laid out on the tables, the blank monitors, the numbered pipes and the reactor trip system in close-up. This lingering tendency to pick out the small details of human presence after the people have left begins to indicate what will gradually go as the whole industry shuts down.

Moving from one institution to another Sattler shows how they are connected both in their day-to-day work and historically. The simulator centre has a relationship with the nuclear power station Zwentendorf in Lower Austria which was completed in 1978. Johann Fleischer and Richard Borowiec tell the story of the referendum which went 50.47% against starting up the station, leading to the end of nuclear power in Austria before it started. The reactor was then converted to a training facility with close links to the Simulator Centre in Essen with workers at German nuclear power plants coming to train. Again the history of the site offers an opportunity for visual reflection. The camera moves through the space inside the containment vessel picking out the remarkable vistas that such a space creates. The guide rattles off the statistics, diameter of 26 meters, 36 meters high.

FIGURE 4.2: A nuclear engineer explains with a glass model what went wrong in the accidents at Three Mile Island and Biblis Nuclear Power Stations. Volker Sattel (dir.), *Under Control* (*Unter Kontrolle*), 2011, Germany. Credofilm, Westdeutscher Rundfunk, ARTE.

The process of shut down is explained along with the nature of the 'biological shield' and the connection with the turbines. The power station, which provides spare parts to five nuclear power stations of the same type built by Siemens in Germany, is shown in poignant images. Each of the parts is pristine.

From a striking shot from inside the cooling tower in Zwentendorf looking up towards the sky, the film moves to a shot of an active cooling tower in a forest in the far distance. It is not explicitly mentioned in the film, but the nuclear power plant Gundremmingen in Bavaria, which houses two boiling water reactors and uses Zwentendorf for spare parts, also has a history connected with accidents. The first nuclear reactor to be built here in 1967 was shut down in 1977 after operational errors following an automatic shutdown. In other words the training given to plant workers is linked to the analysis of this experience when radioactive coolant was accidentally released into the atmosphere. The portrait of Gundremmingen is concerned primarily with the measurement of exposure of workers to direct radioactivity or to the possibility of contamination. In a tradition common to early films about atomic energy, the film shows the machinery designed to wash clothing and to check personnel on leaving the areas of the plant where radioactive materials are being manipulated. But the film also enters into a space where interim storage for spent fuel has been authorized, a licence that has provoked protest and legal action. The castors that contain the fuel are shown to be constantly monitored as they emit the level of radioactivity of a transatlantic flight every hour. While a young man explains the exposure and places his hand on the dark blue surface in a demonstration of its safety, the camera retreats behind the line that labels the other side as the hazardous zone enacting a difference in attitude towards radioactivity.

At this point in the film three organizations are presented, which each have a different reflexive relationship with nuclear energy; the International Atomic Agency in Vienna (IAA), the Institute for Risk Research (IRR) in Vienna and the German Atomic Forum which is having its fiftieth anniversary conference at the Kongresshalle in Dresden. The three institutions also relate to one another reflexively. In the first building, which shares the 1950s retro look of the atomic age, the work done by the IAA on monitoring radioactive material, particularly plutonium and enriched uranium, is explained along with information about which countries are required to submit to verification and the number of incidents involving highly radioactive material. A different use of the camera is inserted here as a visitor to the agency organizes a crew presumably to visit a site for inspection. The forensic use of the camera for the agency's work has already been shown through the comparison of two photographs, which forms the basis of reasoning about the national compliance of nations that are not party to the non-proliferation treaty.

After this, Wolfgang Kromp explains that it is the IAEA that is called in to help in difficult international situations but it has no power. It can criticize nuclear power stations but cannot compel them to improve. His explanations of the risks posed by the waste material produced by nuclear energy production and the long timespans involved offer the first verbal critique within the film of the institutions controlling nuclear power. There is also an obvious contrast brought out by the cinematography between the grand spaces of the IAA building and the cramped rooms inside the IRR located in an older neoclassical building. Meanwhile at the German Atomic Forum it appears to be business as usual as delegates at the trade show talk about persuading women that nuclear energy is safe, a theme that took on prominence within the industry as a response to citizen protests against nuclear weapons and nuclear energy. A lecture on the need to extend the life of power stations booms over images of delegates as they wander around the spectacular building overlooking the Baroque city of Dresden.

The move from this luxurious setting to the nuclear waste repository Morsleben pushes the developing narrative even more obviously towards critique. The sequence is still concerned, however, with the creation of an audiovisual analysis of the space and its role – alongside the power stations, the training institutes, the research institutes and the regulatory bodies – within the system of nuclear power production. A very long lift ride, which appears to be filmed in real time, to the bottom of the salt mine leads to a cavernous space and the sight of yellow canisters arranged in rows, piled two, three or four high, looking nevertheless tiny in the space. Florian Emrich of the Bundesamt für Strahlenschutz explains all the sources of waste, from the military to nuclear power stations and all the types of low level and intermediate waste involved. Then he explains that 2.6 billion Euros will be required to close the site if it is successful in demonstrating that this can be done safely through filling it with salt concrete. Six thousand cubic meters of low- and medium-level waste is stored there. It could have been 18,000 says a voice.

Here the film is again very selective about what it presents in terms of information. It is worth recounting what is left out to demonstrate how disciplined the film is in its strict focus on atomic energy as a system of knowledge. Morsleben is a salt mine, which during the National Socialist period was used as a site to build weapons, including the V1 and V2 rockets. Women interned in the concentration camps in Ravensbrück and Buchenwald were made to work there. In the early 1970s the site was situated in the GDR and used to deposit 500 cubic metres of waste before it had been adapted in any way for use as a nuclear disposal site. It was approved as a site in the late 1970s and in the mid-1980s finally given a permit as an official nuclear waste repository. Low-level and intermediate waste produced in East German reactors, which by that point included Rossendorf, Reinsfeld and Greifswald, was stored there. After reunification Morsleben took nuclear waste from all over the Federal Republic but in 1998 nuclear waste storage at the site was suspended because the caverns were beginning to deteriorate and remedial work was required. While representatives from the Federal Office for Radiation Protection and the German Gesellschaft zum Bau und Betrieb von Endlagern für Abfallstoff [German service company for the construction and operation of waste repositories] speak about the repository, explaining that costs are 'tallied at 2.3 billion euros until closure', the camera again snoops around corners, travels on vehicles and waits in empty spaces.

The brief portrait of the Karlsruhe Institute of Technology is another turning point where it can be seen that there is a distinction to be made between seeing the current nuclear power stations as obsolete and understanding nuclear energy as a whole as at an end. Researchers do not recognize their technology as obsolete and environmentally damaging as they do at the end of Tschirner and Drachsel's *Die Wismut: terra incognita*. Instead, several statements demonstrate a living belief in the future of the industry. The decommissioning of its research reactor and diversification into new fields demonstrate that the industry is not closing down completely. While a man is shown using a remote handling system – an aspect of nuclear work that has not been visible in this film up until now – work on the design of generation 4 reactors is mentioned along with methods to avoid the production of large amounts of new waste of the kind stored in Morsleben. Joachim Knebel offers the view that the vitrification of spent nuclear fuels in Sellafield in the United Kingdom is not a good idea because the material cannot be retrieved.

This account is an important moment in the film with respect to its portrayal of an industry in the process of closure. It questions the thesis that the closure of the power stations represents a historical boundary between the atomic age and the future. The examination of the industry after the decision to close down the energy production is presented in the film as a boundary of a different kind. Traditional atomic energy production, its safety procedures and its production of radioactive waste is shifted to the decommissioning and decontamination of old power stations and to a different way of thinking historically about atomic Germany. The film presents this too as part of the archaeology of atomic energy. What are the old stations good for if not for experimentation and the dismantling and storing and archiving of themselves?

Kalkar, which was to be the first fast breeder reactor in Germany, was developed in response to a perceived shortage of uranium. As such plants were considerably more dangerous than uranium plants and also produced plutonium, a much more fissile material with a much longer half-life, they provoked even more civil protest. Kalkar raised safety questions that delayed its opening in 1985 until it was decided in 1991 not to open it at all and it became one of the biggest investment failures in Germany's history. The site is a rare example of abandonment. The

spaces lit up by torchlight showing wrecked and decaying equipment are remi-
niscent of Tarkovsky's science fiction film *Solaris*. The image of the playground
inside the cooling tower is one of the most striking in the film. The visual analysis
here underlines the clash between the investment decision makers and the population, demarcating the point at which the high level of investment itself failed to
overcome opposition. The children are playing in this extraordinary space because
this point was reached.

The film moves from the power plant that was completed but never produced
energy to a power plant that was never completed. At the time the film was being
made, the power station in Stendal, which was to be the biggest power station in
the GDR, was in the process of being demolished. Never having produced nuclear
energy or taken on fuel it is a simple process of demolition using excavators and
blow torches. Gundremmingen is visited and the events that led to the first accident
in a commercial nuclear power station are told. Three unfulfilled plans: Kalkar,
now a funfair, Stendal now an industrial park, Gundremmingen now a facility for
handling contaminated materials.

As the film moves towards decommissioning activities it emphasizes more the
presence of atomic energy in the radioactive wastes stored in the waste depository
and the interim storage points. The cut from Gundremmingen Block A to the final
site, Greifswald Nuclear Power Station in Mecklenburg West Pomerania, points
to the continuity between the decontamination work in the former and the storage and recycling work in the latter. Here the analysis begins to demonstrate that
the nature of closure is an inherent part of the industry, included conceptually
at the planning stage, but realized in historically different circumstances to those
imagined. 'The dismantling of nuclear facilities, as we have been doing here since
1995, is of course a burgeoning sector of the future', is a comment made by Marlies
Philipp who gives an account of competing for the work of dismantling the nuclear
power stations as they close down. Her voice is accompanied by images tracking
the vast site that housed three nuclear power stations. The plant opened as the
Bruno Leuschner Nuclear Power Station, named for a prominent member of the
Socialist Unity Party and head of the planning and finance committee who died in
1965. An old company calendar is frozen on the date Monday 17 December 1990
'the last day on which electricity was produced by the Greifswald Nuclear Power
Station'. Philipp explains that Rheinsberg, the first nuclear power station to be
built in the GDR, is in interim storage at the site, alongside the first and second
reactors in Greifswald, a reminder that an entire national nuclear industry has
already been shut down in Germany. Phillip's explanation of the process is patient,
like a landowner talking about crops and forests: 'We envision storing them [the
reactors] for fifty to seventy years. Nature does its part to help, as our main nuclide,
cobald-60, has a half-life of 5.3 years so in fifty years the radioactivity will sink

to a thousandth on its own. Some of it can go to the scrap dealer and some will have to go into a nuclear waste repository'.

Control of radioactive material is the job of this archive and the message of the film is that this workforce that does its work in strange plastic suits is needed, along with the spaces to tend to the past, to create and maintain a boundary between us and this past. The film participates in the process of the demolition and reconstruction as archive, going inside the sealed-off pods, and presenting in the form of a documentary study a 'systematic description of a discourse object' (Foucault 2002: 156). It excludes protest in order to discover the 'enunciative homogeneity' (2002: 162), an archaeology, an appreciation of atomic energy.

The final scenes make a humorous return to the Simulator Centre in Essen. After following the escape arrows down a number of corridors, the alarm sequences are set off in a number of its eight simulators that cover all 10 types of nuclear power plant running in Germany. The sound track is a cacophony of alarms that have been heard already, while the control rooms are shown empty with abandoned chairs and flashing rows of light across the panels. This ending for an industry is shown as an abrupt process of abandonment, but the film has demonstrated that there is quite a way to go yet.

Reading radioactive images

Before moving on from this film it is worth spending some time here on the reception and the scrutiny it received. It has already been noted that the funding of the film in 2008 was politically significant in the sequence of elections and decisions made about the *Atomgesetz* and the closure of all nuclear power stations in Germany. Festival reports that include a discussion of the film at its premier in February 2011 at the Berlin Film Festival show how the images were read in Germany primarily as a confirmation of the call for the industry to close. Susanne Messmer for the *Tageszeitung* wrote, '*Under Control*, this close look at the interior of a system acts like a plea for a moment of contemplation. It highlights the absurdity of the effort that was and still is necessary to control this technology and shows how tragic the failure of it is for those who today are still attached to it, full of pride and childish defiance' (Messmer 2011: 30). Julian Hanich wrote, '*Under Control* is a 98 minute film which comes across formally as completely calm and tidy – and yet it pushes the viewer into a wild hot and cold shower of emotions' (Hanich 2011: 30).

A reviewer from New Zealand described how the film was received at its first screening as well as how the film worked differently for viewers outside the particular circumstances of the German political sphere:

Maybe it's because the film is German but the thing is so dry, it's crispy. It's also one of the most objective documentaries this journalist has ever seen. The director, Volker Sattel, barely even seems to have a point of view. He just allows all the interviewees and the pictures to speak for themselves. The reactions of the mainly German audience to the film made it clear though, exactly what they thought. Nuclear power is being phased out in Germany, and it's a pretty controversial subject – every time nuclear safety was mentioned, members of the audience scoffed loudly. And this in itself was fascinating – because one realizes, over again, how much of our own preconceptions we bring to every movie we see.

(Schaer 2011)

After the Fukushima disaster on 11th March 2011, the start for the film in cinemas was brought forward from the autumn to May. A report by Jan Schulz-Ojala demonstrates how the film was at this point read in the context of an extensive media treatment of the subject of nuclear power. Just as Sattel's film was brought forward in the cinema schedules so too a documentary reportage film prepared for the 25th anniversary of the Chernobyl accident by Karin Jurschick was broadcast early by ARTE and ARD. Schulz-Ojala noticed a link between the title of Sattel's film *Under Control* and a clip from an interview with the CSU Bundesinnenminister Friedrich Zimmermann in which the minister stated, 'although we do not have any access to detailed information the situation here is under control'. Schulz-Ojala does not quote the following explanation for that assessment given by Zimmerman 'because we have our data from measuring stations and experts who are able to draw the right conclusions. According to the available data there was and is no danger for us' (Jurschick 2011). For Schulz-Ojala there is only one way to read Sattel's film:

The visually and dramaturgically almost purist concept is nevertheless clear from the first shot: the images should speak for themselves. And they speak – against the continued production of atomic energy.

(Schulz-Ojala 2011)

The reviewer for the *Stuttgarter Zeitung* interprets the film similarly as a strong statement against the nuclear industry:

Because all the actors seem tiny, weak and fallible, and thus utterly out of place as they tinker in the gigantic spaces housing the reactors or with the unreadably complex panels of switches in the control rooms. The visible points to a central problem that the philosopher Günther Anders pinpointed in the early years of the Federal Republic; he spoke of 'antiquated people'.

('Ästhetik der Atomindustrie' 2011)

Katja Lüthge's review for the feuilleton of the *Frankfurter Rundschau* almost accuses the film of deception but recognizes that even though it is not a typical activist film it is 'well thought through' and 'clever'. With extreme scepticism about the good faith of the industry she writes of the beauty of the spaces:

> Because of course Sattel was only permitted to film what would be good for the image of the industry. The cathedrals of atomic fission and the centres for measurement and regulation are suspiciously clean and tidy. Probably the technical teams on shift were told to turn up shaved and in clean freshly ironed short sleeved shirts on filming days. But it only takes a small mean cut to question the beautiful appearance. Concrete plastered over and rusting steel on the outside of the shell, blades of grass pushing through the asphalted access roads: the Atom lobby is not even able to get its own image completely 'under control'.
>
> (Lüthge 2011: 30)

Ulrich Kriest, writing a review, this time for the cinema release, then referred back to the narrative of the reception of the film:

> When *Under Control* celebrated its premiere in the spring at the Berlinale the film drew criticism. The beautiful images spoke of aestheticism, the lack of a position was criticized and it was thought the film had sacrificed too much for its access to the atomic installations. Then Fukushima happened and *Under Control* was literally contaminated. A term such as *Abklingbecken* ('spent fuel pool') would have fallen through ten weeks ago; an ambitious documentary like *Under Control* would probably have found it difficult to find an audience in the cinema. Now this requiem for a technocratic utopia is the film of the hour. The final educational point is kept for the end of the film: the film material itself makes invisible radioactivity visible to the human eye.
>
> (Kriest 2011)

It is striking how reviewers outside Germany in contrast emphasize the film as balanced or neutral. A very positive *Daily Variety* reviewer notes that Sattel 'confounds those on both sides of nuclear-power debate with his monumental film on the life and death of nuke plants, titled, with some tinge of perhaps unintended irony, *Under Control*' (Koehler 2011). Nevertheless a reviewer for the *New York Times* in December had by this point moved to an interpretation of the film as surreal rather than neutral. Despite its title 'An intimate tour of a gleaming German nuclear plant' and its characterization of the film as *The China Syndrome* as it would have been if directed by Frederick Wiseman, it too notes that 'the words reassure but the images unsettle' and 'somehow the happy screams of children whirling above a neutered reactor sound a lot less comforting than they should' (Catsoulis 2011: 10). As an 'intellectually demanding' documentary, Sattel's film thus managed to negotiate the stress of high exposure to a broader audience than might have been expected drawing a spectrum of reactions both to its nature as a documentary and to its purported messages.

The film also manages to maintain its relevance beyond the political context of its first release through its function as a recording, in effect a description of the industry in 2011, at a time when it was clear that all nuclear power stations would close within 36 years with no new power stations being built. It has a taxonomic quality like the photographic technique developed by Bernd and Hilla Becher whose series of images captured the form and variation in industrial architecture – water towers, mine heads, for example. Just as the Bechers sought to capture the images of the buildings in the landscape before they disappeared, Sattel records the nuclear power station still in operation, but also some of the many institutions arranged around and sustaining the power station itself. Sattel's film thus extends the idea of the taxonomy into a more finely grained portrait of an industry including the pressures that have brought about its demise. Thus, although there is a strong elegiac feel to the film it is not truly a work of mourning. It manages to evade the accusation of having something of the pastoral elegy about it, lamenting the passing of the 'good old days' of optimism, by composing an aesthetic tour from the dream through the stages of illusion and disillusion to the reality of an industry that has long phases of development, operation and decommissioning.

An ordinary nuclear power station

Ivy Meeropol's *Indian Point* shares with *Under Control* an appreciation of the nuclear power station as an object in the landscape. Focusing on a single plant and the social world that revolves around it, however, this is a film that contrasts with *Under Control* in its interest in the human stories over and above the architecture. While *Under Control* signals an appreciation of the nuclear age through spectacular shots of buildings that organize individuals into roles, *Indian Point* draws on the memories of its participants and their aspirations to be at the helm of 'Starship Enterprise'.

Indian Point has been praised by critics primarily for the multitude of perspectives represented in the film. Meeropol has described the film as a 'portrait of an issue' rather than a film arguing a particular position. It is character driven: the plant safety officer, the journalist, the activist and the river ecologist amongst others each embody a point of view. The key to the tension in the story is Greg Jakzco, Chair of the Nuclear Regulatory Commission. Without his story 'nothing really

FIGURE 4.3: The nuclear power station situated on the river just outside New York, shown from the air in a shot that celebrates its architectural and infrastructural presence, Ivy Meeropol (dir.), *Indian Point*, 2015, United States. Motto Pictures, Red 50.

happens', as Meeropol put it. The accident at Fukushima, which led to Jakzco's insistence on increasing safety measures in US plants, is described as the 'spectre that informed everything'.

The personal nature of *Indian Point* is in contrast with *Under Control* but it too offers an analysis of an industry that has responded reflexively to historical developments. The film is most interested in creating a visualization of the ties between the characters who are all engaged centrally with the question of the plant's future. As in *Under Control* it is striking to observe the way in which the plant defines the group as a generation. The architecture and equipment of the power station has aged along with the participants in the film. In interview Meeropol has reported that Brian Vangor, probably the most important figure in the film besides Greg Jakzco, appreciated her portrayal of the workers at the plant but recognized that the film was in the end against renewing the licence. Meeropol makes a distinction, however, between being an activist and being a filmmaker. She described herself as 'relieved' and 'reassured' by the way the plant was run. 'It's not Homer Simpson at the controls'. The point, she argues, is that there is too much that is out of the control of the plant workers. The discovery of a second fault line under the plant in addition to the one known was the most serious threat of concern to the Nuclear Regulatory Commission, particularly after the Fukushima accident.

The presence of a gas pipeline running near the plant and another one planned nearby was also a factor, showing in an unusually concrete way the competition between the nuclear power station and the rise of natural gas as the principal source of energy in the United States.

Cold War history

Indian Point was not Ivy Meeropol's first documentary on a nuclear theme. In 2004 her documentary *Heir to An Execution* was a portrait of her grandparents Julius and Ethel Rosenberg who were convicted of spying for the Soviet Union, sentenced to death and executed on 19 June 1953. The film is an autobiographical account of Meeropol's attempts to connect with family members in order to find out more about what her grandparents were like as people. The refusal of any of them to adopt the Rosenbergs' young sons is the strongest evidence of how oppressive the McCarthy era was.

This early Cold War story about the balance of power between the United States and the Soviet Union is a long way from a contemporary local struggle over the licensing of a nuclear power plant. Yet both are legacy stories of the atomic age. A comparison between Meeropol's approach to her grandparents' story and her insistence on allowing the many perspectives on Indian Point to have space shows her two documentaries are connected by the slow processes of connecting memory to history. The story of the Rosenbergs has been told by historians many times. Meeropol's retelling in the form of an autobiographical documentary took the step of connecting it to the present via the living descendants, showing how the slow release of information is also connected to the lasting trauma of a period when the development of atomic energy was at the centre of the new world order. The reasons for the slow release – de-classification, *perestroika*, a sense of personal release through time from the obligation to secrecy – all play a part in *Heir to an Execution*. The trauma of past experience – and perhaps a sense of shame – is shown to be the factor that can last the longest.

Ordinary atoms

In his vision of 'reflexive modernization' Ulrich Beck argued that in the 1980s citizen-initiative groups gained a political power of their own: 'They were the ones who put the issue of an endangered world on the agenda, against the resistance of the established parties' (Beck et al. 1994: 38). Beck describes their achievement as a 'thematic victory', that is, during the Cold War they managed to create a new focus on the environment both in the West and in the East by taking to the streets and demonstrating. Beck interprets the turn to direct action, which is pursued not only by environmental activists but also by nationalist movements, as a struggle to create a new kind of politics to stage consensus. He describes this process as disruptive and leading to what looks like an inconsistency in individual political allegiances as long as the terminology of politics in the old order of industrial modernity is used – words such as 'right and left, conservative and socialistic, retreat and participation' (Beck et al. 1994: 21). What emerges in Beck's description in the mid-1990s is a 'sub-politics' in which 'agents *outside* the political or corporatist system are allowed to appear on the stage of social design (this group includes professional and occupational groups, the technical intelligentsia in plants, research institutions and management, skilled workers, citizens' initiatives, the public sphere and so on)' (Beck et al. 1994: 22). This is a politics from below which reduces the power of the institutions to implement their policies. As already seen in the film *Uranium Drive-In* a complex of different groups were in conflict but ultimately the deciding factor was cost and the rise of an alternative source of power production.

While this form of sub-politics can be discerned in *Under Control* in the visits to the various institutions in Vienna, in *Indian Point* it is fully developed in a controversy local to the city of New York playing out in the national context of nuclear energy production. It is not of any inherent interest outside the community represented except that instead of laying out the arguments for and against closing the plant, Meeropol explores a model debate that is repeatable elsewhere. What is at issue is the purported ordinariness of nuclear power. Can the documentary portray a nuclear power station as an ordinary building in an ordinary commuter neighbourhood? Why should the need to have iodine pills and emergency evacuation plans in the cupboard be considered extraordinary? Other types of plant also have evacuation plans, after all. If the nuclear power station opens up to public scrutiny will it overcome the public relations issues and gain the important support of local citizens in the forums designed to include their voice?

Meeropol has described the significance of access to the power station as the most important factor in whether the film could be made. Once access is given, as with *Under Control* the film is a record of a moment in the history of this place and this workforce. It does not need to be 'read' as it represents on its surface all that it is necessary to know about the issues and their outcomes. It is an ordinary documentary. Does it make sense to claim for it anything extraordinary simply because of the presence of nuclear fission? Is there nothing more to it than curiosity and nervousness about the interior of the industry, a kind of acousmatic presence that will be revealed as benign once the curtain is drawn back?

This is the key question posed by the film. While introducing the power station as having an aura enhanced by the dissemination of leaflets detailing safety precautions and the evacuation plan, in and around the plant the filmmakers are at pains to show the regular everyday life of the nuclear power station and its workers. As the film follows Vangor into the radiologically controlled area, he introduces himself in a voice-over, explaining that his employment at the plant was the result of the accident at Three Mile Island in 1979 after which new regulations required a qualified engineer at all plants. The sound track to the film is nevertheless conventionally sinister as an exterior shot opens to the containment building and shows men working in white suits. As in *Under Control* the attention of the camera operator wanders into corners and behind screens picking up radioactive hoses and caution signs. While Vangor explains the production of electricity from the fission process, where 'the magic happens' the camera is focused on men looking into the fuel pool and chatting. The editing of Vangor's explanations with shots of the interiors and exteriors of the plant both coordinate the information and situate it as an everyday workplace with rules and procedures guided by the knowledge of risk. Generally it allows the nuclear power station itself to come out into the open as 'not like Homer Simpson'. The film carries out its job of showing Vangor and his colleagues responding to the additional scrutiny brought by the Fukushima Daiichi accident including new training using the simulator that Vangor explains as a stressful process, like being on a battle field. Fukushima is duly added to the Three Mile Island routine. It also records the visible aging of the plant and the approach to fixing or replacing the deteriorating or breaking items so the plant could 'run for a very long time'.

All is revealed to be OK but as in *Under Control* the film also expresses the meaning of the power station for the workforce, emphasizing pleasure in its efficient working. A sequence with cine film shots of a tour in 1966 shown, as in *Uranium Drive-In*, as a frame within the frame, provides an opportunity for Vangor to represent a heritage view of the plant, an alternative history in which it is remembered as part of a new world of low emissions and clean energy. The DVD has additional material that features Vangor engaged in his hobby as a local historian. His comment, 'I always wanted to be Captain Kirk', demonstrates the orientation of children's toys and media around the new roles envisaged for them in the 1950s and 1960s: 'You sit in the control room at Indian Point, I sit up on the CRS desk, I have my ATC operator, my BOP operator. It's basically the same thing'.

Although the film is generally supportive of this story, it moves towards critique at certain points. Vangor explains: 'It still amazes me. I walk into the containment building or I walk into the control building or the control room and I look at the print row circuits and it absolutely amazes me that they thought of all these things. This plant could run way longer than thirty years, way longer than fifty years. I don't see why we can't just continue to inspect every place and repair as necessary'. At the same time, long shots that show an attractive blue-and-yellow coloured space are followed by close-ups that show patched and shaking pipes leaking steam.

As a film, then, *Indian Point* gives the nuclear power station workforce the opportunity to represent itself as ordinary, benign and competent and to express the desire for the old plants to continue producing energy. Meeropol's camera is permitted to enter the power station, to see the reactor floor, to observe refuelling and repairs just as Geyrhalter's camera was permitted to enter the Chernobyl power station guided by the safety officer there.

Community of resistance

The rest of the cast represent a debate, which is shown as unmoved by showing that the plant is operated competently. Returning to the image of the plant itself and its position on the river, the environmental journalist Roger Witherspoon offers a running commentary on the gap between the point of view of workers in the nuclear industry and the general public, a gap that by 2011 has become part of the everyday: 'For those who work in the industry this is a safe plant. For those who don't work in the nuclear industry there are risks you don't want to live with' (Meeropol 2014).

Meeropol's portrait of Marilyn Elie, a retired teacher and activist, is almost unique in being a sympathetic film portrayal of a woman campaigning against nuclear energy. In several films, media clips of Helen Caldecott are inserted to critique what is often portrayed as a hysterical point of view. Even a film made by her niece, Anna Brionowski, *Helen's War: Portrait of a Dissident*, doubted whether her strident Cold War arguments of the 1980s could be translated into the twenty-first century (Brionowski 2004). Elie makes a distinction between being a journalist and being an activist, a distinction that is important for her relationship with Roger Witherspoon. The story of this relationship is an important factor in the film primarily because of the principled way in which Witherspoon supports activism as the expression of genuine concern, an action of the alternative public sphere working on the politics within the public sphere.

Interviews with Phillip Musegaas, attorney for the Riverkeeper Organisation, an environmental group that was founded in 1966 by a group of fishermen, provide opportunities to see the plant from the point of view of the Hudson river. In the same year that the Riverkeeper Organisation was founded, the environmentalist and singer Pete Seeger founded Clearwater to raise money to build a traditional boat called a Sloop which used to be common on the river. These two organizations and the Indian Point Safe Energy Coalition appear at various points in the film – along with the environmentalists' song 'this world is made for you and me' – so that parallel to the history of the plant the history of the environmental movement is told. Musegaas comments at various points on the regulatory procedures and on the impact of the plant on the river. The debate about the water quality sampling programme is one of the points at which it appears that the power plant may have to close.

Thus far, the characters or, to put it in the terms of the social documentary, the social actors, represent a local struggle to use the existing rules either to maintain or close the Indian Point nuclear power plant. As Beck argued in *Reflexive Modernization* the mechanisms for inclusion appear to have produced a form of congestion leading to a paralysis that is persisting into the twentieth century as communities have waited for the power stations to reach the end of their operating capacity. The question of extending licences, a political issue in Germany, is portrayed in *Indian Point* as a sub-political struggle that reaches a critical point with the accident at the Fukushima Daiichi power station. As the reactor in trouble was an early version of the Boiling Water Reactor supplied by General Electric, Toshiba and Hitachi, the issue also concerned the US Nuclear Regulatory Commission. The visit of its head, Greg Jaczko, to Fukushima features in *Indian Point* as it did in *Containment*, making the images of the triple disaster continuous with his visits to US nuclear power stations and the issues raised about the storage of nuclear fuel there. After his declaration 'Nuclear power stations should only be allowed to operate if we can really guarantee that we will not need to have these kinds of large scale evacuations' the film cuts to Indian Point putting the power station within the same space as the Fukushima Daiichi plant.

In 2019 Jaczko published a book about his experiences as regulator (Jaczko 2019) describing how he came to believe that nuclear power is a 'failed technology' after experiencing the Fukushima disaster. He also deals in the book with the various accusations levelled at him, particularly those put in Congress, which caused him to resign. The film, which also gave Jaczko a platform to state his position, defends him by including archive television footage of Senator Barbara Boxer, chair of the environment and public works committee in California, who says when she investigated, the women at the NRC said Jaczko was fair and treated everyone equally. She goes on to say 'I am disturbed because what I think it's about is something entirely different. I think it is about how fast we are going to move on safety at our nuclear power plants. There are a lot of people that don't want to move expeditiously. Please, all of you, sit down and do what's right for the country'. Two points are significant about the film representation of Jaczko's resignation with cameras present. Jaczko is presented in the film as a father with a young child. As such he is portrayed as part of a generation that sees the nuclear industry in a different way compared with Vangor's generation. In his book Jaczko refers to the significance of his youth several times. One such account is of his meeting with the Japanese Minister for the Environment Goshi Hosono. There is a disagreement about the need to use water to control the fire at the Fukushima Daiichi plant. The use of water would increase the amount of radioactive material washed into the ocean, traditionally a particularly sensitive political issue in Japan. Jaczko relates that Hosono referred to his own age at the time – 39 – implying that this was a reason why making the decision to use water would be difficult for him. Jaczko writes: 'A rush of emotion went through me. He was just one year younger than I. In my professional life, and I suspect in his, there was no one else who knew the pressure of making such profound decisions at this age. The challenge of confronting a sceptical industry and bureaucracy – made only more sceptical by our youth and apparent inexperience – was something he and I could truly understand' (Jaczko 2019).

Both *Indian Point* and *Under Control* produce film portraits of the nuclear industry at a moment of institutional paralysis. These portrayals can be understood as political insofar as they make visible a potential future of closure and begin to rehearse the emotions that such a future would involve. The directors make it clear in interview that they do not support attempts to continue with the industry but they also express a desire to support the people working in it by making it possible to view it without *pro* and *contra* rhetoric. Through the process of conceptualization, research, filming and editing, each film produces an analysis. *Under Control* can be understood both as an archaeology, in Foucault's sense, and as an aesthetic of the industry in Germany. Through its tour around and between the spaces of the nuclear industry, power stations that are operating, that have closed or that have never opened, its research institutions and its international bodies, its waste and recycling facilities, the film outlines the positivity that gives the industry its dynamic and sustains it into the future despite operating in the country with the most active protest community in the world. *Indian Point* is a sketch of a long local dispute that explores how and why each position has been maintained over a long period, in part defining the lives of participants. Through its encounters with participants and the portrayal of them as social actors positioned within an ongoing drama it opens each attitude to the possibility of empathy and so, like *Uranium Drive-In*, participates in a form of virtual reconciliation. Both films are anti-nuclear, in that they imagine a future world in which nuclear power production will have been established as a theme for museums and adventure parks.

5

New nuclear reflexivity:
Rob Stone's *Pandora's Promise* (2013, USA) and Mika Taanila and Jussi Eerola's *Atomin Paluu* (*Return of the Atom*, 2015, Finland)

Introduction

In his essay on the future of politics written in the early 1990s Beck envisaged the future of reflexive modernity, driven by the polluting and risk-laden side effects of industry, as increasingly plagued with paralysing conflicts 'between and inside the institutions, parties, interest groups and public spheres of all types' (Beck 1992: 48). Such conflicts are only possible to capture in observational documentary when the penetration of the camera into different institutional spaces created by governmental, non-governmental and protest groups has been enabled. As has already been seen, however, in *Uranium Drive-In*, *Containment* and *Indian Point*, the adversarial positions do sometimes also play out in the United States in broadcast media as well, making it possible to contextualize local struggles over the future social relationship with uranium.

In this chapter, two films are brought together in which the politics of the future is focused on more nuclear energy production rather than the necessity for dealing with its past. The films discussed thus far have represented the existential aspects of the encounter with ionizing radioactivity as a sometimes abrupt and sometimes very gradual process of learning and adaptation, forcing the need for greater transparency, and necessitating acceptance of an increasing role for measurement and monitoring in the management of everyday life. The conjunction of scientific precision with a simple way of life in the zone around Chernobyl has produced a particularly resonant new vision of the future. It is a delicately balanced image, however, in which politics is largely excluded in favour of the effort to bridge gaps in understanding. In the case of arguments about investment in the future of nuclear energy production, the politics have played out more contentiously as has been seen in films about uranium milling (*Uranium Drive-In*) and the prolongation of existing nuclear power stations (*Indian Point, Under Control*), or have been in the background of the debates about nuclear waste (*Into Eternity, Containment*). *Pandora's Promise* to be discussed here in this chapter is specifically focused on making the case for new nuclear energy technologies, while *Return of the Atom* follows the story of the building of a new power station in Finland.

These two films engage with radioactivity as a political problem so that when it comes to on-screen representations it appears in a different way. It seems important for the question of nuclear communications to understand what happens to the logic of the visualization of radioactivity when the focus is not radiological or health oriented, but where stress is laid instead on the idea of it as a natural phenomenon. The use of the word 'natural' in the context of energy production has developed particularly in relation to natural gas, the current main competitor in energy solutions besides coal, with its own body of documentary films extolling (Hefner 2009, Mellot 2012) or lamenting (Fox 2010) the phenomenon of fracking or alternative drilling technologies. Despite the evidence that the industry has attempted to naturalize itself (Gwin 1990: 80–83), the persistent image of nuclear energy as artificial and high tech is negative next to the idea of a fuel that is pumped out of the ground in a more tangible way, however messy, and so a context has been created in which it makes sense to highlight yet more the fluctuating levels of natural background radiation in different parts of the world. The organization of social life around the presence of radioactivity becomes in this context something to be ascertained and highlighted. Measurement in these films too is a critical part of the encounter, but not as part of a horror scenario so much as prompted by curiosity, sometimes part of the 'dark tourism' explored in the opening chapters, sometimes linked to tourisms organized around natural phenomena. The focus in this chapter then is on Rob Stone's enthusiastic return to the history of nuclear engineering and on Mika Taanila's fascination with *Science Noir* and the first law of thermodynamics (Taanila 2013).

The promotion of radioactivity

Pandora's Promise is a pro-nuclear film directed by Rob Stone, who is known, amongst other things, for his work *Radio Bikini* (1987), a compilation film like the well-known *Atomic Café* (1982). While *Atomic Café* cut clips of the US military manoeuvres experimenting with nuclear warfare together with the children's *Duck and Cover* animations, *Radio Bikini* used promotional military footage made during the testing of atomic bombs over the Bikini Atoll in 1946, intercutting safety assurances made to the public via radio with images that clearly contradicted them.

Stone uses similar editing skill in *Pandora's Promise* to represent the complex history of nuclear energy, but this time supporting the future of the technology via the testimonies of five converts and two nuclear engineers who were part of the first generation of development. The film was endorsed by investors with an interest in nuclear power and its role in energy policy. It is distributed by Vulcan Productions, a company founded by Paul G. Allen, the co-founder of Microsoft. Richard Branson is named not only as an investor but also as executive producer and some Silicon Valley investors are also listed (Dolan 2013). New research into nuclear energy that is featured in the film is also connected to investors in them such as Bill Gates' backing for a technology called a traveling wave reactor that uses depleted uranium as fuel.

Pandora's Promise was first broadcast on CNN in November 2013, presented as controversial, and accompanied by a personal defence by the director (Stone 2013b). Stone and the participants in the film are also listed as co-authors of an ecomodernist manifesto that sets out its approach to nuclear power as follows.

> Nuclear fission today represents the only present-day zero-carbon technology with the demonstrated ability to meet most, if not all, of the energy demands of a modern economy. However, a variety of social, economic, and institutional challenges make deployment of present-day nuclear technologies at scales necessary to achieve significant climate mitigation unlikely. A new generation of nuclear technologies that are safer and cheaper will likely be necessary for nuclear energy to meet its full potential as a critical climate mitigation technology.
>
> (Asafu-Adjaye et al. 2015)

Although from this description *Pandora's Promise* sounds like a promotional film rather than a documentary, the film also represents an intriguing historical investigation into the relationship between environmental and nuclear protest. In the wake of the Fukushima disaster Stone confronts a number of environmental activists who have decided that nuclear power is part of the solution to climate change and takes one of their number to Fukushima a year after the triple disaster. For this chapter it is this use of location shooting that is significant along with the extensive use of Geiger counters to compare radiation in different places as a kind of on-location persuasion. When it comes to the promotion of nuclear energy, the film revisits and represents all of the arguments that the industry has pursued with respect to the development of improved technologies in a post–Cold War environment, the safety records, radiological health, the production and storage of waste and the threat to world peace. Ultimately, it puts its support behind continued research, in effect, a continued faith in the possibility of finding a way to use nuclear science. Archive material is used extensively to illustrate what the talking heads recall, and visits to different locations around the world offer information on the fluctuations in background radiation in different parts of the earth to compare with that in Chernobyl and Fukushima.

The second film in this chapter is entitled *Return of the Atom* (2015), a Finnish film directed by the artist and documentary filmmaker Mika Taanila and his collaborator Jussi Eerola. This film focuses on the first new power station to be built in Europe after the accident at Chernobyl. The Finnish plant Olkiluoto (OL3) is the moment of return presented in the film that premiered in 2015. It is an extraordinary mix of experimental rock video using time lapse footage of the power station being built, and satirical documentary investigation into the community around it. All the glamour of the nuclear renaissance is celebrated in spectacular images of gigantic cranes crouching over the containment vessel as it rises from the ground to the electronic music of the Finnish duo Pan sonic. At the same time, this rebirth is contextualized with footage of the local community and the construction workers that belies the hyperbole.

When researching for this book I went on a coach tour around the construction site of Hinkley Point C in Somerset, the second new nuclear power station in western Europe since Chernobyl and the first nuclear power station for twenty years to be built in the United Kingdom. This experience brings out something of the sense of *déjà vu* in the contemporary nuclear building projects, which, far from representing a new era, appear very much like the old one, only bigger. Driving around the 'biggest building site in Europe' (Guillaume 2018) and peering out at the men peering in their turn down at the steel mesh for the concrete foundations was rather like walking into one of the many historical films I have been watching for this project. Indeed episode nine of a company film magazine entitled 'Home and Away' (available to watch on the Scottish National Library website) has very similar scenes of site workers building what is now the decommissioned Hinkley Point A. Made for the Australian firm Babcock and Wilcox (Steam) Ltd between 1954 and 1961 to promote its work for the Electricity Board, each magazine was a mix of engineering milestones and local colour. Episode nineteen, made around 1960, presents a short section entitled 'Three of a Kind: A Story of Atomic Power Progress' and features Hinkley Point. Star of the show is a goliath crane, described as a 'spectacular structure [which] will straddle an entire reactor house and be capable of handling loads of up to 400 tonnes'. Meanwhile in 2019 the tour guide to Hinkley C is promoting the project for EDF. Yet larger numbers involved in this engineering venture are presented: the numbers of jobs created, the amount of concrete poured, the size of the boring machine to create the tunnel far out into the Avon Estuary. In January 2019 the crane, the SGC-250 (also known as Big Carl after the engineer Carl Sarens) is about to arrive. It is capable of lifting 'an astonishing 5000 tonnes' and its first deployment is to Hinkley Point C.

A special sub-genre in television documentaries relating to large engineering projects or 'mega' projects has developed in the new millennium using digital technology. Computer-generated modelling, time lapse photography, and the filming of highly radioactive spaces and objects by remote controlled or robotic cameras are ways in which the future is first projected and then realized not only as a process of cleaning up after the catastrophic past, but also as a plan to build new and better facilities. Nuclear energy has provided subject matter for this genre mainly in the form of containment and decommissioning projects. Films such as *Sellafield Demolition* (2009), *Supersize Grime* (2011), *Fukushima Robots in Hell* (2016) and *Inside Chernobyl's Megatomb* (2017), some showing images flashing from radiation interference, are full of superlatives about danger, epic time spans, quantity and size. The appeal of the films derives partly from a vision of a world of robots – the three heroic Fukushima robots in hell sadly 'die' during their mission – and partly from the achievement of the engineers who work out what needs to be done. Even the massive budgets they command are celebrated for their epic size. New build projects, however, have largely been restricted to company websites, making *Return of the Atom* an unusual exception.

Mika Taanila's work is best understood in this context of the history and present of atomic energy projects. *Return of the Atom* presents a humorous comment on the contrast between the promotion of the new power station built in Finland, Olkiluoto 3, and the technical difficulties that have repeatedly held up the project, increasing its budget considerably. The film was planned and shot over a period of eight years and so covers the shift from the nuclear renaissance to the period after the Fukushima accident. Through its montage of footage of the epic project of building Olkiluoto 3 with documentary footage of the community of largely Polish construction workers, as well as of the nearest town, Eurajoki, it reflects both on the power station as a 'mega project' and on the situated day-to-day existence of the people in and around it.

Media inserts supplement the documentary footage. A number of advertising slots, *50 months in 300 seconds, Olkiluoto 3, The EPR Uncovered*, and *AREVA Funkytown Commercial*, represent the upbeat promotion of the project by the lead contracted company Areva. Television broadcasts from the Finnish programmes *Daily Review, Western Finland*, a show called *MOT Buying a Nuclear Power Plant*, and a selection of daily news broadcasts, provide a running commentary about the media response to events. A satirical tone emerges out of different aspects of the project intercut with old genre films that reflect on the history of nuclear energy in the region. A rarely seen US animated film *Three-Two-One-Zero* directed by M. Clay Adams from 1954, a Soviet animated film *Zdravstvuj atom!* (*Hello Atom!*) directed by Lev Milchin from 1965, a US remake *Gammera – The Invincible* of a Japanese Monster film from 1966 partly set in Finland and a GDR

Western *Die Söhne der großen Bärin* (*The Sons of Great Bear*) from 1956 give the tone to the progress or lack o f progress of the project.

High seriousness and satire in contemporary nuclear films

The discussion of these two films then is focused on an emotional reckoning attempting to understand the present situation for nuclear energy through references from the past. The documentation of radioactive spaces in *Pandora's Promise* is embedded in stories that are driven by the individuals' account of their developing opinions and dreams. The participants have all contributed to debates about the future of energy through writing and activism in the past and want to be part of a revival of nuclear technology in future. Significant in this is the progress of their personal understanding of radioactivity that has been shaped by the imaginative representations of the past.

In his research for the study *Speak No Evil* Louis Gwin set out how the requirement for the industry to engage in the communication of nuclear safety came into conflict with the promotion of nuclear energy. Writing about the new legislation in the United States introduced by the Atomic Energy Act in 1954, creating new roles for its Atomic Energy Commission in permitting private industry to exploit nuclear science, Gwin states that, 'in effect, Congress was asking the commission to *promote* atomic power with one hand and, through licensing of reactors, *regulate* it with the other – a pattern that would have important implications for the industry's later risk communication efforts' (Gwin 1990: 50, original emphasis).

Although this situation is noted by the current generation in the early twenty-first century in *Pandora's Promise*, in the context of climate change they also express their sense of having been duped by the fossil fuel industries' interests too, which, it turns out, funded campaigns highlighting the dangers of nuclear power stations. *Pandora's Promise* thus destabilizes both the promotional and protest-driven history of film representations of the nuclear industries by demonstrating that the promotional culture that developed during the Cold War is inherently unhelpful as a way to assess the real costs and benefits of any energy form. The representation of the zone around Fukushima might seem to be a way to reinsert the consistent threat of uncontained radionuclides but the film puts this into question also, reviving both the history of 'naturalizing' radioactivity in ways that Gwin has also pointed out were tried in the past, as well as focusing on women and young people as particular targets in need of conversion.

Return of the Atom also presents an unstable debate, but in this case it is its geopolitical position both in the far north and between East and West that creates the disturbance to the prevailing sense of normality. Some context for this can be found in the project HoNESt, funded by the European Commission's Horizon 2020 and EURATOM, which produced a set of twenty reports on European countries as part of a programme to 'understand how societies have engaged with nuclear energy, including how the nuclear energy sector has engaged with societies over the course of the past 60 years'. The passage on Finland's history, characterized by its position between the USSR and its European satellite countries in the East and the United States and its allies in Europe in the West, is oddly contradictory, providing a suitable background to the satire communicated by *Return of the Atom*. The first two sentences set the scene for the whole report:

> The interaction between nuclear energy and civil society in Finland has developed since the 1950s without major political and ideological clashes. There have been public debates, demonstrations, and an intellectual counter-culture lobbying against nuclear energy at national and local levels.
>
> (Michelsen and Harjula 2017: 10)

The very densely edited film *Return of the Atom* echoes the different directions in this summary, bringing out the exoticism of the very northern location and the unusual density of electricity lines there, as well as the small local efforts at protest and at ascertaining whether the bedrock is watertight, where the geological waste repository (represented in the film *Into Eternity* discussed in Chapter 3) is located. Radioactivity as a phenomenon is accompanied by the electromagnetic field produced by the density of the electricity lines. What comes out of the film is not an argument against the power station so much as a sense of the incongruity of the life building up around it, not only in the present but also progressively since the beginnings in the 1950s. The film poses questions about the logic of the development of modernity itself, expressing Taanila's consistent engagement with technology as part of human fantasy. The film expresses his approach to nuclear energy which he has described in interview as follows:

> Nuclear power as a means of producing electricity is a rather old notion, if you think of the rapid technological innovations of our time. In a way, it is a relic of the past that is nearly 60 years old. But it is perhaps still a good choice in many ways; uranium is not yet an outdated element and financially it appears to remain very lucrative.
>
> (Taanila 2013: 41)

Pandora's Promise *and the nuclear conversion story*

Just after the opening to the film, *Pandora's Promise* presents a number of environmental activists and writers watching a moving image of one of the explosions at the Fukushima Daiichi power station (Figure 5.1). The extended shots of them looking at

FIGURE 5.1: The participants – Michael Schellenberger, Gwyneth Cravens and Mark Lynas – are shown watching the explosion at Fukushima on a screen before discussing their support for the development of new nuclear energy technologies, Robert Stone (dir.), *Pandora's Promise*, 2013. United States. Robert Stone Productions, Vulcan Productions.

the screen are important for the film and for the concept of radioactive documentary, in that they include the image as a major influence on the imaginative understanding of nuclear energy and nuclear accidents. The point of *Pandora's Promise* here is the attempt to use the frame within the frame to question the messages conveyed by mass communications. The nuclear industry is presented as the victim of ignorant journalism. Protest is also represented as wrongly motivated. The opening shot of the film, for example, shows a campaigning group and their poster – Shut Down Indian Point Now! At first it might seem as though the film will be opposing the closure of the power station but this is not the point of this scene. Rather it is about framing a particular kind of campaigning against nuclear power represented in the figure of Helen Caldicott who, the film wishes to show, spreads misinformation about science. At the end of the film Caldicott appears again but by this point she is rendered completely mute and shown in slow motion while her voice is replaced by one of the pro-nuclear campaigners who states that the next generation will 'understand nuclear'. This and many other aspects of the film show that the film as a whole is intentionally partisan. The face watching the screen represents the individual thinking person versus the anti-nuclear media.

The environmental activists and writers Stewart Brand, author of the *Whole Earth Catalogue*, Richard Rhodes, author of *The Making of the Atomic Bomb*, Gwyneth Cravens, author of *Power to Save the World*, Mark Lynas, Earth First activist and Michael Schellenberger of the Breakthrough Institute are bona fide political activists and writers embodying Beck's class of social actors who make a career of environmental politics. In belonging to such a community they have all experienced criticism for their support of nuclear energy and so find that they need to explain their reasons, not to an oppositional group outside, but to their own community. They have, in a sense, to go against the success of the environmental and anti-nuclear movements. There are two aspects of the film that are interesting to look at in the context of this study. The first is the significance of personal encounters with nuclear science. The second concerns the location shooting, not only in the zone around Fukushima but also in other radioactive spaces.

The reframing of the history of nuclear communications continues as the stories of the individual participants become embedded in a broader history of nuclear energy development and production. Like the participants in the documentaries *Indian Point* or *Under Control*, they themselves demonstrate how they have been acted upon by the history of technological development. They articulate how their emotions as children and young people have been engaged by the fear of nuclear war or nuclear accident, how they have been swayed by both education and protest. The test presented by the film is for them – and by extension for the spectator – just one further emotional and cognitive test to add to the many that have already been part of growing up in the atomic age.

Mark Lynas is the participant who travels to Fukushima and it is his statements that demonstrate the logic of the film. While the other participants' memories are recounted in part through media clips, Mark Lynas himself is shown in them as a 'hard core activist' and part of a media event organized by Earth First, with the slogan 'no compromise in defence of mother earth'. He explains his behaviour was motivated by his identity rather than by reasoning: 'I was against nuclear power because I was an environmentalist'. Embodying environmentalism as both anti-nuclear and anti-fossil fuel, his separation of anti-nuclear campaigning from environmental campaigning can thus be understood as an attempt to reverse the union noted by Barnouw in his *History of Documentary* (see page 9).

The inclusion of Gwyneth Cravens as one of the five converts seeks to recompose the story in a different way. Speaking about her childhood and about motherhood her contribution rebalances the gender bias set up by the unsympathetic portrayal of Helen Caldicott. Cravens takes her story back to her childhood when she experienced learning about nuclear physics as exciting and was encouraged in her interest in science. Her point is about going back to re-embrace this initial positivity which is the overall message of the film. She talks about the Disney television series 'Our Friend, the Atom' (Luske 1957) a programme produced for children as part of a series called *Tomorrowland*, which is also discussed by Gwin in his account of the public relations history of the nuclear power industry (Gwin 1990: 86–87). The inclusion of a clip from this film inaugurates the interweaving of media history and witness testimony that relates very specific individual stories to the public sphere. In 'Our Friend, the Atom' the story of atomic research is turned into a fairy tale in which the genie explodes out of the lamp like an atom bomb. Aladdin manages to get the genie back into the lamp by tricking him. After granting Aladdin three wishes he is let out again and so the story goes into the atoms for peace programme.

This children's film demonstrates some of the issues for media representations of nuclear energy. On the one hand, it is an excellent example of how the history of science is communicated to children as a sequence of people handing down and developing ideas. The history of atomic research is taken back to Democritus and his newly invented word *atomos* to describe the indivisible thing out of which everything is made. John Dalton is described as a scientist who went back to Democritus for ideas. Becquerel's experiment putting uranium on a photographic plate is animated as are the Curies, Einstein and Rutherford. In explaining how fission works, however, the slowing down of events through slowing down the film is conflated with the reduction of neutron emissions, creating the strange idea that the film intervenes in reality. A film of a room of mousetraps going off all over the floor is slowed down with the explanation: 'Our mousetrap explosion can be slowed down with the aid of a slow motion camera. As you can see the chain reaction is now spread over a longer time.

The illustration of Craven's memories with archive film creates a slightly uncanny effect when she describes how, as an enthusiast for science, she was impressed when Admiral Hyman G. Rickover came to give a speech and demonstrated the atomic submarine the USS Nautilus with a model. This is a cue for more archive footage this time of what looks like this very demonstration.

Later in the film, archive footage of the accident at Three Mile Island in 1978 as well as clips from the feature film *The China Syndrome*, a speech by actress Jane Fonda in 1979 about utilities executives and profit motives, and a huge rally in New York against nuclear power is accompanied with commentary from Craven who explains that she conflated nuclear power with nuclear weapons at that time. The decision not to open Shoreham Nuclear Power Plant which was completed in 1984 but was never put into full operation turned on the evacuation plan which was never agreed with local communities and the state. Cravens describes how she, and many women, felt protective towards their families over the issue but also argues that the community was swayed by adverts against the nuclear power plant placed in newspapers by oil companies afraid of competition from nuclear power.

The inclusion of a speech by Margaret Thatcher made on November 8, 1989 to the United Nations on the subject of climate change brings in another female voice. The speech as printed and released by the No. 10 Press office can be found on the Thatcher Foundation website (Thatcher 1989). It is well-known that Thatcher was strongly in favour of nuclear power and in this speech she indeed stated that one of the solutions to the many environmental problems listed involved nuclear power. It is surprising that the extract from her speech does not include her statement that nuclear power: 'despite the attitude of so-called greens – is the most environmentally safe form of energy'. The speech as a whole is strongly in favour of international cooperation on the basis of scientific work, setting out various contributions made by the United Kingdom to institutions for measuring and finding out more information about the changing atmosphere and species depletion.

In *Pandora's Promise* Thatcher's speech is cut and pasted in a way that does not preserve the integrity of the footage. It changes the order of points while giving the impression of continuity, partly enabled by the evenness of Thatcher's delivery, and reduces the sequence to a statement about the seriousness of the situation:

Long shot of Thatcher at the podium of the United Nations Assembly:	'The difference now is in the scale of the damage we are doing. We are seeing a vast increase in the amount of carbon dioxide reaching the atmosphere'.
Cut to close up of Thatcher accompanies cut to earlier statement in the speech:	'It is mankind and his activities which are changing the environment of our planet in damaging and dangerous ways'.
Cut back to long shot accompanies cut to later statement in the speech:	'Change to the sea around us, change to the atmosphere above, leading in turn to change in the world's climate, which could alter the way we live in the most fundamental way of all. That prospect is a new factor in human affairs. It is comparable in its implications to the discovery of how to split the atom. Indeed, its results could be even more far-reaching'.
Cut to view of the audience listening and to later statement in the speech:	'We can't just do nothing'.

The comparison between the discovery of atmospheric change and the discovery of the atom is intriguing. Thatcher's speech is concerned with building the political institutions and funding for cooperation on the basis of scientific research and seems to demonstrate complete support for government-funded science and political negotiation over business, stating: 'We should always remember that free markets are a means to an end. They would defeat their object if by their output they did more damage to the quality of life through pollution than the well-being they achieve by the production of goods and services'. The reference to the splitting of the atom is, then, about the progress of human knowledge as much as it is about politics and economics, linking it to Eisenhower's 'Atoms for Peace' speech, also delivered at the United Nations Assembly, on 8 December 1953 which was concerned with 'the fearful atomic dilemma' (Eisenhower 1953). Thatcher's speech is about the fearful dilemma posed by the new knowledge produced by scientists she cites from the Polar Institute in Cambridge and The British Antarctic Survey.

The connection is hence insightful despite the cuts and leads into visual graphics that represent scientific modelling relating to climate change (and also despite the extraordinary elision of the struggle between Thatcher and Arthur Scargill as head of the National Union of Miners, the miner's union striking over the closure of mines in the United Kingdom). Simon Taylor has written about the process of restructuring nuclear energy, which began with an electricity privatization white paper in 1988 (Taylor 2016). He writes:

> On 8 November 1989 Margaret Thatcher made a speech to the United Nations on the role of nuclear in reducing the risk of global warming. The following day Wakeham pulled nuclear completely out of privatization and stopped all plans for new nuclear stations pending a nuclear review in 1994.

He summarizes the change in the evaluation of nuclear energy:

> The reputation of nuclear power in the UK in 1989 was at an all-time low. The promises, made over many years, that nuclear would become economic were revealed as at first hopelessly optimistic and then dishonest. The older stations had worked reliably but the advanced reactors had continually failed to operate properly. The CEGB [Central Electricity Generating Board] had the appearance of an organization that had decided nuclear was the future and had fixed and distorted the numbers to make it seem viable. Only the scrutiny of the private sector had brought all of this to light.

After the Thatcher speech and simulation of climate change the film cuts to the British activist Mark Lynas and his two children and wife walking to the park and so does not contextualize the problems with the British nuclear programme and in particular its problems with Fast Breeder Reactors that become important for the argument about renewal in *Pandora's Promise*. The story of how Shellenberger and Nordhaus lost faith in and broke away from the environmental movement is interwoven with Lynas's story. They both put forward the idea that the renewable and efficiency argument is deceitful. It is remarkable to see the extensive energy debate that had been taking place all through the 1970s, 1980s and 1990s, including the 1997 Kyoto protocol, and into the new millennium, radically cut in this way. The personal approach of the film and its focus on personalities tends to represent activism as preoccupied with reductive arguments.

Stewart Brand's account of his childhood reinforces the sense of an intense engagement between individuals and government-promoted mediated accounts of the bombing of Japan followed by nuclear tests. Brand describes how he, as a child, responded to the film *Duck and Cover* (1952) and the routines at school where children practised going under their desks. His description of it as 'pretty personal' and of having nightmares is reinforced by Stone's montage of different archive materials from the period to accompany what he has to say. Again the very close relationships between his memory and the archive material create a slightly uncanny effect. Brand, however, is the participant who creates the link between the stories of the environmentalists and those of the nuclear engineers who persuaded Brand to consider nuclear energy as a solution to the decarbonization of the energy.

The younger Michael Schellenberger is perhaps the most conflicted of the participants as he describes how it was his anti-nuclear parents who brought him up to see the school visit to a new nuclear power plant as a propaganda campaign. The archive footage of the new power plant again reinforces the story along with the inclusion of a clip from *The Simpsons* which is unusually recast as propaganda rather than as humour. Richard Rhodes describes his conversion to nuclear energy as coming about through talking to physicists: 'the pioneers of nuclear energy […] who carefully explained again and again until it finally got through my head why it wasn't what the anti-nuclear activists felt it was, believed it was'. Through this statement Rhodes, expert on the contemporary history of the atom bomb, becomes the cypher for the archive footage and interview material with Charles Till, who explains the development of reactors to produce power in the 1950s. A key argument in the film relates to the view that the wrong kind of nuclear reactor – the light water reactor was chosen for development.

A visit to Chernobyl and Fukushima

Lynas' visit to the Fukushima exclusion zone is accompanied by a Geiger counter that shows on-screen the level of radioactivity as he walks about in a white protective suit. The phrase 'I am having a wobble' is a sympathetic response to the situation that demonstrates the authenticity of the test. At this stage in the film the reading on the Geiger counter is not explained although the commentary states that the carpark is the most radioactive area. Later a sequence with Geiger counter reading is central to a naturalization strategy as it is seen in different places in the world demonstrating the levels of background radiation. All of the readings are in microsieverts to enable comparison beginning with Guarapari beach in Brazil which is famous for its radioactive sand. It is shown with the highest level at 30.81 microsieverts per hour, while Los Angeles is shown at 0.09 microsieverts, Paris is 0.10, Kiev 0.17. In Chernobyl the counter is held up showing 0.92 while in Fukushima it is 0.18. There is no specific commentary about these numbers beyond an introduction that explains them as an attempt to be consistent about background radiation as both a natural and artificial phenomenon. Variation itself appears to be the point as well as the idea that it has less bearing on the health of the environment that might be assumed from reporting on Fukushima. Lynas' voice is heard over the sequence in the Chernobyl exclusion zone putting forward the same arguments that were used to distance the worldwide nuclear industry from the accident in the Soviet Union, particularly through the claim that the Chernobyl reactor was 'inherently unsafe, primarily designed to make plutonium for bombs'. Lynas is honest about his lack of knowledge about radiation before he began looking into nuclear energy and so what we hear is a beginner's guide tailored to a complex argument about knowledge and representation.

The film presents glimpses of the return of people to Chernobyl and we see an image of Andrei Rudchenko, who participated in the film *Pripyat*, chopping wood outside his house. Another sequence of arguments is produced that the anti-nuclear movement has been misleading the public about the effects of the nuclear accident. Helen Caldicott is brought in again as evidence of misinformation while the report prepared by the Chernobyl Forum, a group of UN agencies plus the governments of Belarus, the Russian Federation and Ukraine is quoted to refute her claims (The Chernobyl Forum 2006). The numbers of deaths attributed to the accident by the WHO and the report produced by the IAEA are given – deaths of workers brought in to deal with the situation from acute radiation syndrome are put at 28, and 19 further deaths are recorded but not attributed to the accident. Deaths in the general population as well as damage to unborn children are put at zero. All together the points made construct an opposition

FIGURE 5.2: A Geiger counter is taken around the world to show how background radiation varies in different places. Here it is held up in the exclusion zone around Chernobyl power station. This is clearly intended to contrast with the use of such measuring equipment in protest films, Robert Stone (dir.), *Pandora's Promise*, 2013. United States. Robert Stone Productions, Vulcan Productions.

that is focused on deaths and mass cases of cancer, which can be refuted so that the acknowledgement of Chernobyl as a tragic accident can be also owned by a pro-nuclear position.

When the film then turns to Fukushima and returns to Lynas' visit he saves the film from crass arguments about numbers by pointing out that these are not appropriate. Lynas instead focuses on the problem of communicating what is safe to the general public in terms of radiation in the environment. Here no distinction is made between radiation, which is indeed everywhere, and the scattering of radioactive particles across the landscape, which is the effect of nuclear accidents that creates a permanent increased health risk. This means that the nature of the dangers being discussed and the kinds of clean-up operation that are required are not actually communicated by *Pandora's Promise* at all. The major debate in the nuclear institutions about safety culture, which was seen as the primary cause of the accident at Fukushima, is not discussed either. The idea that the lack of an open and transparent approach to risk and risk procedures played a role is left out. The argument that a more open and liberal organizational structure that acknowledges public concern is appropriate for this kind of high technology is not included.

It is difficult at this point to take the demonstration that the risks of nuclear accidents have been exaggerated seriously as the film becomes more driven in its representations by its opposition to anti-nuclear campaigners. A number of decisions made with respect to nuclear institutions are presented as motivated by the mistaken politics of the left. The closure of the Argon National Laboratory for advanced reactor development, which was working on the Integral Fast Reactor, is presented by Richard Rhodes as a 'mistake' merely based on opposition to Republican projects.

This presentation of a series of personal point-of-view statements demonstrates the difference between the montage of archive footage and a film presenting current opinion. The isolation of the statements undermines them. Stewart Brand visits Yucca Mountain and in the opening to the tunnel states that 'Science fiction is what we were playing out at vast expense at Yucca Mountain' nevertheless making the claim that the mountain was not opened 'for political reasons'. Brand describes how he went to see where nuclear waste was being stored 'back of the building in the parking lot' and a Geiger counter is duly brought out to show how low the levels of background radiation are. Nuclear waste is presented as minimal and unproblematic in every case. Craven states, 'Nuclear waste is not an environmental issue. It is not an issue that I as an environmentalist am concerned about'. Schellenberger nullifies arguments about the economic cost of nuclear simply by stating that infrastructure costs are cheaper than solar and wind. A renaissance in reactor design is proclaimed by Brand, supported by the very fact of investment by Bill Gates. Small modular reactors as local power sources are mentioned as the first glimpses of the future of nuclear power.

The declared purpose of the film, in its attempt to save nuclear energy as a low carbon asset, is to create a belief that the dangers of nuclear power production have been exaggerated, mainly through the demonstration of a new community of distinguished participants in the film who are willing to represent the arguments. The close connections between their life stories and the history of nuclear energy mediated through moving images are also means to connect a collective story about optimism followed by anxiety which could become hope for the future once again. However, the sense that the film itself is attempting to solve all the issues by overriding the effects of a history of faulty communication strategies puts a strain on it, which becomes more and more palpable as the film and the arguments advance. As an expositional film, it fails ultimately through its inability to recognize itself as a reflexive response to the cumulative problems being created by the globally diverse production of nuclear energy as well as the other forms of energy production – fossil fuels and renewables – which it attacks.

At the same time, however, there is a further thread that is not about the environmental community but about the pioneer engineers who developed the technology for the nuclear industry from the late 1940s with some undeveloped possibilities along the way. Leonard Koch and Charles Till tell their stories accompanied by archive footage, reconstructions and animated diagrams. This strand, which is engaged with the highly controversial fast breeder reactor programme, represents another about turn by the environmentalists who rejected it in the 1990s when these reactors were considered the future particularly because they could recycle some of the highly radioactive waste produced by other reactors. The transportation of this material from Japan to Europe or from the continent to the United Kingdom became the focus of many violent demonstrations. The objections again are not covered in the film but some of the more positive history of the technology is related, and it is put forward as making a return, reflecting current thinking in research in the context of decommissioning, nuclear disarmament and further decarbonization. Just as the idea of nuclear waste disappearing forever underground is attractive, so too the diagram suggesting that it can be shrunk to tiny amounts that last only eight hundred rather than a million years provides the viewer with some optimistic moments.

Pandora's Promise then enters the fray, examining the history of nuclear communications in audiovisual media through the lives of people influenced by it. It does not critique or reflect on this history of communication so much as bring it forward as evidence, arguing for a continuation of nuclear energy as a process of evolution that goes back and tries out the roads not travelled the first time around. The audiovisual history is accepted along with the statements of the participants as part of the evidence of what happened in the past. The film circulates as such online as an intervention, an influencer, continuing to offer its arguments to viewers exposed to all kinds of other points of view.

Return: Atomic time

Return of the Atom, a film with an inscrutable tone, is, in contrast with *Pandora's Promise*, characterized by puzzlement. At the heart of it is the sequential documentation of the building of the Finnish nuclear power station Olkiluoto 3. Each segment of time-lapse footage represents progress that nevertheless is also a failure to maintain the promised schedule. The projected date for completion is continually pushed further into the future. As the expectations are shifted each year so the attitude towards time in the film also shifts. To begin with, the tempo is swift and management proclaims the new era of nuclear construction as efficient and well planned. As things get bogged down, the significance of speed is downgraded and the value of stamina emphasized.

The film itself, being a time-based medium, works with different kinds of documented time. The on-screen sequences vary, with the slowest being still takes of the countryside in winter and the fastest being the time-lapse sequences of the construction site. The time lapse, however, does not really represent the fastest passage of time as the whole film is divided up by a series of seven intertitles giving a month and a year, indicating that between the periods of filming there are varying jumps in time: October 2004, August 2005, June 2006, September 2007, August 2008, November 2009, ending with March 2011. Then there is also the archive footage from the building of the earlier reactors on the site. These represent a jump back in time to a television report in 1974 when the construction licence was awarded for the first Olkiluoto nuclear power plant, with further archive footage showing the building sites before the first plant connected to the grid in 1978. The film also includes computer-generated images projecting the building project into the future. Images from animation films, science fiction films and a low budget western represent fantasy worlds outside time, but are also strongly marked stylistically as 1950s- and 1960s-era genre films.

As in *Pandora's Promise* the reorganization of the human social world through uranium is captured in *Return of the Atom* as an historical process conveyed through archival representations, but there is a different approach to these and their meaning. In *Pandora's Promise* the past was represented through the archive as contingent and leading to error because of the political and economic context in which decisions were made. In *Return of the Atom* the past is represented as mysterious and difficult to reconstruct. Accompanying the variations in time are highly volatile shifts in tone. These come about through a process of editing that often follows leads in the language used in interview that are themselves puzzling. Portrayals of the exciting new world of atomic physics and nuclear energy production in archive footage are also selected with a view to showing how they too expressed the mystery of it all. It sets out with an inspired choice of a rarely seen US animation about subatomic physics directed by M. Clay Adams who was best known for his television series *Victory at Sea*. The voice-over text accompanied by pacey abstract animations emphasizes in a whimsical way the newness of the knowledge. The relevant lines are applicable to the project of building the third reactor in Olkiluoto: 'It is very simple and different. Similar and different. First there are cosmos, suns, stars, planets, comets, and meteors, of which man knows very little. Then there is the solar system, part of which is Earth. Molecules are a combination of 92 elements'.

The cut from this to a coast full of construction workers being transported to the site marks an abrupt change of pace contrasting the day-to-day physical reality of a large engineering project with the lightness of the idea or image of atomic energy. The coach, however, also features an up-beat commentary that links it with the animation: 'You're building a new, third reactor. Let's see what you are building for us. Olkiluoto 3 (OL3) is the first nuclear project in Western countries after the Chernobyl disaster (1986)'. The promotional material with its computer-generated images and statement 'It will be the most powerful power plant in the world' reconnect again with the animation.

The variations in time and tone stringing the years of the project together mark this film out as a raucous ironic study of the mentality of the large mega project that is nuclear energy, going beyond the debate itself to become a study of the strangeness of human life. As there are no exterior shots outside the island of Olkiluoto and the town of Eurajoki, the film creates an enclosed world visited by the arrival and departure of aircraft and coaches. It recalls Kafka's fragmentary novel *The Castle* with the existing power plant standing for the inaccessible castle to which the village – Eurajoki and the housing built for the construction site workers – is beholden. Various items imposed on the village, such as the large billboard welcoming newcomers to Eurajoki with the words 'the most electrified town in Finland', represent a kind of updated version of Kafka's village. Taanila used it as the title of his video installation about 'life in a nuclear town' using footage shot for the film. The installation premiered at the dOCUMENTA in Kassel in 2012 and is described by Kati Kivenen as about 'the relationship between technology, people, and nature' (Kivenen 2013: 76). In a discussion at the beginning of the film, a resident explains that everyone either works for the power station or has a relative working there and explains the lack of resistance to it with a Finnish saying: 'The branch where you sit, you never cut it'.

Although a review of the film in *The Hollywood Reporter* describes the film as 'a black eye for the nuclear-revival movement' (DeFore 2015), the film is even handed in its satire.

It creates several threads through the film that return and develop as the years pass by. As already mentioned, the town of Eurajoki itself is introduced right at the start as the village to the castle. As the film progresses the Mayor shows the filmmakers around the well-provided facilities of Eurajoki town hall, including the cupboard where the Geiger counters are stored. Archive footage of the power stations being built in the past, which is black and white even though it is only in the 1970s makes the link between the building of that period and the buildings in the present. Rauno Mokka, Vice President of TVO (Teollisuuden Voima Oyj) is a star of the film. His role as chair of the hockey team, his tendency to be shown eating and his deep voice engaging in a friendly way with questions put to him means that he survives the satirical treatment well. His statements about the minimal impact of the project on wildlife are nevertheless set against the story of a woman who attempted to protest against nuclear power in the 1980s. She is shown as a young woman demonstrating and also in the present looking back on her younger self portrayed in the newspapers. She shows a poison letter she received and explains how she eventually stepped down her opposition after ten years.

Access to the workers on the site is at first via the welcome, then via the religious services and finally through filming of the separate housing facilities and entertainment. Sakari Leppännen the pastor provides some access to the community and is himself also part of the collective portrait of eccentricity as his sermons attempt to create some connection between Christian worship and the construction of the nuclear power station. The comments such as his thanks to the foreigners 'who have come to help Finland get a new power station', or their thanks for 'being in an independent country, not slaves, able to earn money and live', or comparisons with the birth of Jesus as 'true light coming into the world', are disconcerting for the way they are framed within the conventions of collective prayer and are yet relevant to nuclear power. Later in the film a more down-to-earth portrait emerges through shots of the rather rudimentary cooking facilities along with the workers passing time fishing in river and then later still enjoying night club entertainment in which the female performers dance with fire.

The spokespeople for the engineering project on behalf of the corporations Areva and Siemens, who are building the site for the Finnish nuclear energy company TVO get a similar treatment to executives portrayed in Achbar and Abbot's documentary film *The Corporation* (Achbar and Abbott 2003). Their statements are accompanied humorously by media inserts that stand in for the filmmakers' imaginative response to their words. As Bernard Léger of Areva explains the importance of the project to build the first EPR OL-3 and explains its safety features designed in the wake of the attack on the Twin Towers in New York in 2011 and with the meltdown of the reactor core in Chernobyl in mind, those two events are shown on-screen in a way that is not reassuring. The statement 'I currently believe in the return of nuclear power' is accompanied by a Russian animation that, like the one that United States used earlier, adopts the jolly breathless tone: 'Atom – an almost magical, inexhaustible source of energy. Artificial sun. Atomic vessels, star ships. Conquering oceans and space. Atom'. The insertion is motivated by the description of the Finns as 'avant-garde'. Later the country is praised for being a 'beautiful democratic example' in contrast with other countries that are unable to make rational decisions because of their form of thinking and debating. Uwe Kaufmann Siemens gets similar treatment as he talks about increasing energy use and climate change. The arguments are undermined by the production of a marzipan model of the power station followed by melting glaciers and computer-animated polar bear images.

The delays to the project began very quickly at the foundations stage so that by August 2005 documentary images of the site in trouble are smoothed over by a speaker who compares Areva with a very heavy train. This and the description of the schedule as 'aggressive' is a cue for archive images of a train crashing into a car on the track somewhat similar to some tests carried on to see if nuclear waste containers could survive such events. As an image of a man shredding paper is shown, the speaker expresses his belief that they will catch up and explains that he himself is off to the United States to launch the new reactor there. The image of that plane taking off underlines the sense that the management engagement is superficial.

The portrayal of environmental campaigning against the project is equally satirical. The new protestor is a power station employee campaigning against his company. He is often shown in the dark typing long complex documents into his laptop computer, the light shining on his face. A local farmer's worries about the effects of the electricity generation and high-voltage cables in the area are inserted at times through the fading out of voices as electronic buzzing gets louder. Archive film is also used to comment on the organized activities of the protestors. A 'Nuclear Madness Info Center' appears in a forest setting and is followed by some more statements from the US animation: 'We are not yet in touch with reality. The future will be more strange and not more familiar'. As satellite pictures are discussed along with the question of the energy used to deal with the waste and the use of helicopters to terrorize the local people, the film cuts to scenes from a children's monster film *Gammera – The Invincible* in which the monster is destroying a power station. This re-edited version of the Japanese original begins with the landing of an American research group in a place that sounds something like Olkiluoto. The collection of evidence in the form of samples and statistics and the demonstration that there has been some seismic activity in the past through uncovering the strata of a local outcrop of rock is not shown as irrelevant but the isolated activity of an individual gathering and arguing in the face of a large bureaucracy is looked at askance, again in a manner similar to Kafka's heroes with their hopeless revolutionary intent. Evidence is heard in an official process but it again appears estranged and senseless.

The time-lapse photography of the reactor core being built demonstrates the continued progress of the project. Footage of explosions carried out by the blasters also punctuate the film at strategic moments. Shots from the containment vessel up to the sky as well as shots from the tunnel maintain the balance between the scale of the project and the scale of the universe called on as the provider of energy. An event outside all of this ends the film in March 2011 with the triple disaster in Japan. The film reports through a series of intertitles that Siemens withdrew from the project after Germany decided to drive down all its nuclear power plants. It is noted that 'Olkiluoto 3 is nine years late on schedule' and that 'AREVA and TVO are claiming billions for arbitration from each other' but that 'TVO plans to build an OL4 plant unit'. The power station is at time of writing not expected to go online before 2021 and the Finnish government has withdrawn plans for new building.

Conclusion

For all their differences, both *Pandora's Promise* and *Return of the Atom* respond to evidence of the particular path that nuclear power generation has historically taken with critique that is respectively explicit and implicit. *Pandora's Promise* sets out the possibility that a different path could have been and could still be taken that would rescue nuclear power from its current predicaments and turn it into part of a solution to climate change. *Return of the Atom*, representing the difficulties confronting the building of a new nuclear power station, is ironically friendly about the past, but cannot engage with such utopian optimism about the future. The film turns a reflexive recording of the project into a reflection on the uncertainties it represents, even referring to a thought experiment in statistical physics as a way of reflecting on the uncertainties that the discovery of subatomic particles brought into the natural sciences. The subtitles to a section included in the trailer read: 'Try to prove 10 squared -6. The chances are one in a million that I'll be 100 meters underground in one second. These are very difficult concepts. The chance of a meteorite hitting here could be 10 squared -10. We should fear it [laughs]'.

Both films bring archive material in to demonstrate the affective mishmash that has contributed to the confused emotions and attitudes that nuclear energy inspires. As an advocacy film, however, *Pandora's Promise* continues to demonize protestors and elevate nuclear scientists so long as they are the ones with the right solutions. As a satirical treatment *Return of the Atom* portrays the madness of an era through the illogic of a contemporary project. A film that tends to straddle the gap between artist's film and documentary it might be understood as a reflection on the human condition in the twentieth century, plagued by an awareness that the optimism of the past has led to multiple crises in the present.

Beck's argument that the only way forward is to persist with the same reasoning and the same reflexive responses in the hope of gradually honing modernity raises innumerable questions about what the future might be. As Pontus Kyander puts it in his analysis of Taanila's *Science Noir Trilogy*, most representations of the future show it as something that is past, a dystopian vision of an industrial treadmill that has been replaced by an image of failure, aging and decay. In Taanila's work in contrast the future is kept open and mysterious in part through the ways in which the products of science, including visual media technologies, turn out differently to expectations, also producing human behaviour that differs from the projection:

> this becomes a meditation not only on science, but on time and how we ourselves move and change with the technologies surrounding us, adapting the news of today and forgetting what only a short time ago was the bright, shining possibilities of tomorrow. Just like in the start of film experiments, the medium continues to be new and full of possibilities, and without us noticing slowly recedes into the shadows of redundancy and oblivion.
>
> (Kyander 2013: 96).

In the spirit of the reflexivity it includes film itself in all its forms – documentary, animation, science fiction genre, educational and so on, indicating that documentary moving images themselves are also an overly hyped and emotional vehicle for public debate, perhaps better for some other purpose instead.

Conclusion, or the endlessly reflexive archive:
Tim Usborne's *Inside Sellafield* (2015, UK) and Mark Cousins' *Atomic: Living in Dread and Promise* (2015, UK)

At the beginning of the BBC documentary *Britain's Nuclear Secrets: Inside Sellafield*, Jim Al-Khalili, Professor of Physics at the University of Surrey, and well-known presenter of the radio series *The Life Scientific*, describes himself as extremely excited. This is, in fact, quite a common state for a TV scientist to be in on camera, but this time it seems genuine. He is about to go – as the title of the programme indicates – *Inside Sellafield* – to see the most toxic place in the world. In decades gone by the presenter of such a prospect might have been concerned, outraged, sarcastic, but the tone in this document of the new millennium, in keeping with the many documentaries made about the megaprojects of science and engineering, is none of these. It is enthralled. The toxicity of Sellafield is something to be seen, a wonder, and what makes it even better is that it not easy to get to see it.

In this chapter some of the threads of the study will be brought together in a discussion of two films made for television about British nuclear history. Tim Usborne's *Inside Sellafield* is a BBC production that focuses on the central issue for the current industry and for its past. Using archive material that was consciously made 'for posterity' from the late 1940s but kept secret at the time, it marks the time between the initial circumstances in which the industry developed and the current focus on decommissioning and waste processing. It works hard to make the place and some of the processes carried out there visible with a script that celebrates what has been achieved there but also recognizes the lack of 'thought for the future'. Radioactivity or the treatment of radioactive objects is what the place trades in. Its workforce handles it, keeps it secure and processes it into manageable objects for the future. National wealth is invested in it by necessity and a

126

documentary such as *Inside Sellafield* has a role to play in its public relations. Through its explanations of nuclear fission, the history of the Cold War and its interviews with contemporary workers at the site, it attempts to bring together the 'wonder' of the science programme with the aura of World War II and Cold War history to address a diverse audience drawn to the programme from many different political positions. Within the national context its reflexivity relates both to the question of new nuclear power stations and the location of a deep geological repository. The sense conveyed that the task of dealing with the past is in hand is critical to these projects. It is a radioactive documentary in taking the camera into spaces at Sellafield that matter and that give it the claim to be 'the most toxic'.

The difficulty of entry to British nuclear sites was the first aspect of the new atomic industry to be documented on film. The press, with particular journalists such as Ronald Bedford the 'atom reporter' for the *Daily Mirror* or James Cameron for the *Picture Post* and the *Express* or Robert Jungk for the *Guardian* playing a lead role, had to battle with government D-notices – places designated restricted to journalists – to get to tell the public anything about developments that were being authorized to spend very large sums of money. The earliest newsreel item about the Atomic Energy Research Establishment, which was to develop both military and civil applications of atomic energy, was focused on 'Didcot Atom Village', which was presented as a sleepy place bemused by the leap into atomic age taking place on its doorstep. Indeed, the images captured by the British Pathé newsreel cameras are striking in their contrasts. The village in Oxfordshire (not Didcot) of the 1940s is tiny and rural, with its low brick buildings and church at the centre, in the midst of fields of grazing sheep and swaying corn. The appearance of a settlement of prefabricated housing, populated by young modern women, makes the strongest of contrasts as they are more visible than the long low buildings inside the former military airfield. But a central theme is the difficulty of getting inside. Using a style that is meant to imitate the old villagers – who had been invited to a meeting in the village hall about the scientific work being carried out – the commentary notes the arrival of 'strangers' who, however, are not let inside without being checked: 'From the office boy to the biggest boffin of all they are stopped at the gates. There's a guard, not a village constable. Security police they call them. [...] All day long lorries come and go. They are stopped at the gates too. Surely they don't think there's a spy in there?' (British Pathé 1947)

Al-Khalili's excitement at being admitted to the Sellafield site in Cumbria in the North of England joins this long-filmed history of high security surrounding British nuclear installations whether civil or military. It took a year to get through the security procedures for the filming to take place. And yet, his journey inside it, as with the newsreel item about the village near Harwell, is also an act of using moving images to break down the secrecy of this industry. It is a paradox that the routines of going through security, and the process of blurring out and obscuring areas in the complex that are sensitive, are part of what attracts attention and excitement belonging as it does to the world of what Alvin Weinberg once labelled a priesthood. In their popular book *Nukespeak* Hilgartner, Bell and O'Connor sought to set out the effects of the initial context of military high security on subsequent nuclear communications in the United States, connecting it to George Orwell's warning novel *Nineteen Eighty-Four*. *Inside Sellafield* is an attempt to get past this history too to present the report of a physicist who wants to see how the industry is approaching the problem of decommissioning and decontaminating the nuclear reactors and their sites. Usborne's programme concentrates on making the issues as visible as possible, recreating Otto Hahn's experiment splitting uranium atoms 'for the first time on TV' (Usborne 2020).

Toxicity as a national challenge

Inside Sellafield, which immediately provoked some strong criticism in *The Ecologist* (Lowry 2015), was broadcast as part of a small season on BBC4 in August 2015. Named 'BBC Four Goes Nuclear', it marked seventy years since the bombing of Hiroshima and Nagasaki. Mark Cousins' film made for BBC Storyville, *Atomic: Living in Dread and Promise* was another film broadcast, made specifically to mark the occasion, reflecting more directly on the anniversary. A compilation film with a soundtrack by Mogwai, *Atomic* is a montage of archived newsreel, information films, television documentary, docu-fiction and independent documentary. Although it is ostensibly divided up into sections, it does not have a commentary, nor does it follow a precise chronology, but instead moves in cycles around a number of themes heading towards the present. These are in effect the gradations between the dread and promise indicated by the title. The images cover both the official and the unofficial narratives present in the history of British nuclear culture as Jonathan Hogg has covered it decade by decade in his book on the subject (Hogg 2016).

It is difficult to evaluate the stance taken up by the film *Atomic* such is the density of the archival curation. The impression it leaves behind is of a grim history paradoxically driven by processes of scientific and social discovery. The sobering archive film of Hiroshima after the atomic explosion is balanced by extracts from *March to Aldermaston* (Knight 1959), a collective film showing the growing public resistance to the hydrogen bomb in the 1950s. Extensive passages shot in Eastman colour of the tests carried out by the British in Australia are included along with the washed out colour television news footage of the arrival of medium range missiles in the 1980s, marking an historic moment in the history of protest in the UK. The community actions against the movement of nuclear waste around the country are juxtaposed with extraordinary footage, created as part of a public relations exercise by BNFL, of a nuclear waste train crashing at full speed into a concrete barrier. Extracts from Peter Watkins' celebrated anti-nuclear documentary banned by the BBC, *The War Game* (1965), are shown repeatedly along with snippets of civil defence films. The footage also includes nuclear discoveries and the efforts at the BBC to cover the Campaign for Nuclear Disarmament acknowledged even in the volume *Nukespeak: The Media and the Bomb* (Aubrey 1982), a knowledgeable and passionate collection of essays published at the time. Extracts from an information film, *Sound an Alarm* (1971) appear as punctuation marks. The head of a man peering out of a hatch into a newly devastated world turns all that follows into a comment both on what has been done and on what has been avoided. It is footage that flows by meaning different things to different generations, signifying nothing more and nothing less than the entire stressful history of the Cold War with its momentous discoveries and its nightmares.

These two programmes focus on the history of atomic energy in a single state – the United Kingdom – and commemorate it in very different ways. The national context of the industry and the national broadcaster together make them more clearly part of a public reflexive process bringing footage of radioactive spaces into the public sphere in a way that is designed to be inclusive. Both of them have reflexive qualities, in that *Inside Sellafield* must be understood as part of the need for public understanding and debate about the nuclear legacy in the United Kingdom. *Atomic* is equally a response to contemporary concerns, marking an anniversary as a moment to take stock of the changing relationships between the United Kingdom and Japan in particular. Although *Inside Sellafield* is focused on the problem in hand, it introduces the history of it using a sequence of extracts from archive films that go right back to the beginning of the British atomic project. Footage of a pipeline being built out into the Irish Sea was classified at the time it was shot. Windscale, Calder Hall, the T.H.O.R.P.E plan for an international nuclear waste recycling business are all part of the story, also featuring in Cousins' *Atomic* so that the two films are linked by the emphasis they place on nuclear history as something that needs to be dealt with both culturally and physically. After the sequence in which Al Khalili enters the site, *Inside Sellafield* moves on to a sequence that uses archive footage to tell the story of the British project to build a nuclear weapon. At the end of it a cooling pond is shown, where, as Al Khalili comments, there are 'clues that reveal the story of Britain's entry into the nuclear age'. Archive footage is shown of the cooling ponds as they were at the beginning of the 'atomic age' represented in the promotional film *Atomic Achievement* (Reeve 1956) before they are shown as they are today.

This is one of the infamous Sellafield storage ponds. The size of eight Olympic swim-ming pools, it's the largest open nuclear pond in the world. For about a decade, between the mid-1950s and 1960s, this five metre deep water was used to store a huge range of nuclear waste, all sorts of experimental nuclear fuels, highly radioac-tive isotopes, hazardous irradiated debris and contaminated leftovers.

(Usborne 2015)

This text demonstrates an awareness not only of contemporary scientific prob-lems, but also of a humanities-oriented concern with historical materiality, find-ing a crossover in the idea that the murky objects lurking for some 60 years in the cooling ponds at Sellafield embody and here also represent the 'physical history' of Britain's nuclear past. By filming it in the present as a radioactive space, the programme creates new footage, a new radioactive documentary to pass down to posterity. At the same time, at the end of the program Al-Khalili expresses his opinion that there is a future role for nuclear energy and that the experiences of the past should be used to further the research of the future. As has been seen, this is a theme that is implicit in many recent films about cleaning up nuclear sites, which demonstrates that they are not just reflecting on the past as part of a reckoning but rather that they are reflexive, part of an ongoing process that is still respond-ing to contemporary issues and taking them into the future. The toxic superlative that has become part of the new mega project documentary – the mega radioac-tive documentary perhaps – is communicating continuity with the past for a new generation that is to deal with the ongoing legacy.

Archives and affect

A similar intertwining of reflexivity and reflection, which, however, also incor-porates the world of music and art cinema, is at work in the archive compilation *Atomic: Living in Dread and Promise*. Cousins' film cuts images together but does not create out of it a simple narrative that points towards the future. It is not a structural experimental work like Bruce Connor's *Crossroads*, a nuclear collage made in 1976 using found footage of US nuclear tests, which generates both a sense of awe and reflection on the sense of awe. It does not satirize it either as did *The Atomic Café* in 1982, which cut US civil defence films made for children together with nuclear military exercises. It also does not create a forensic indictment as did Stones' *Radio Bikini*(1987) cutting denial on radio together with evidence on film, nor does it use the archive for complex historical-cultural analysis as in Adam Curtiz's episode of his television series *Pandora's Box*, 'A is for Atom' (1992). In the *Guardian* Phil Hoad compared the film negatively with these others, arguing

FIGURE 6.1: An archive image of the storage ponds at Sellafield taken from the film *Atomic Achievement* (1956) to link to contemporary images of the nuclear waste still stored there, Tim Usborne (dir.), *Britain's Nuclear Secrets: Inside Sellafield*, 2015. United Kingdom. British Broadcasting Corporation, Artlab Films.

that it 'falls short as straight documentary or visual poetry'. He notes that Cousins is a film historian and praises him for his work for television in that field but this 'cine-essay' he describes as a 'laborious archival pasteup' and criticizes the fact that the film is neither analytical nor poetic (Hoad 2016). These qualities, however, take the film away from the reflective qualities of the essay and make of the compilation a more direct response to the material. Like *Return of the Atom* it creates a circular movement, reflecting on the continuous back and forth between memory and history that resides in the archive in the extended encounter of old with new kinds of visualization created over the course of 70 years.

A discussion of a sequence of images in *Atomic* demonstrates quite simply the use of the archive to reorder not factual history but emotional history. Footage of the bombing of Hiroshima moves from propaganda about Japan to filmed images made by the US army of the flight to the bombing site, cross-cutting with images of daily life in Japan. Images of the bomb dropping and exploding are followed by a montage of atomic explosions in tests, part of the official publically available image of nuclear war. The pan across the centre of Hiroshima in ruins, used in early newsreels and internal army information films to report the attack, follows this montage. It is an image that has been extensively discussed because of the lack of any human presence. As Susan Courtney has pointed out, it 'shows not a single dead body, nor anyone visibly wounded or sick' (2018: 216). The images of human damage that then follow in *Atomic* – particularly an image of a small shivering child – puts suffering back in as it was recorded by Japanese reporters in the aftermath of the explosions in Hiroshima and Nagasaki which was suppressed by both Japanese and American censors. *Atomic* represents not only the horror of atomic war but also the contemporary emphasis on the visibility of different perspectives no matter how painful they might be. In this collage of archive footage the film creates a documentary and affective record of the memory of Hiroshima that reflects 70 years of gathering and assimilation of images. It constructs what now seems to be a more appropriate approximation of terrible human hostility and suffering.

In the post–Cold War era, the problem of environmental contamination and the need to invest in remediation has been accompanied by a process of remembering and debating the historical legacy of all the nuclear industries from different perspectives. In Germany the film *Wismut* is an early example of this process as it has been captured in documentary cinema. Comparing it with *Uranium Drive-In* demonstrates that it is not only German citizens who are having to think about the future in relation to the shared atomic past. The period covered in this volume has, however, also been decisively marked by the triple disaster in Japan, which has brought a sense of urgency and relevance to the present moment. The scale of the accident at the Fukushima Daiichi nuclear power station is only surpassed by that at Chernobyl in Ukraine so that the two accidents now form a body of knowledge and images that realize the fears set out by early anti-nuclear campaigners such as Robert Jungk, whose work *Brighter than a Thousand Suns: The Fate of the Atomic Scientists* was re-released in 2020. *No Man's Zone* and *Pripyat* are films that focus on the people affected by the accident who provide a highly focused perspective that demonstrates the importance of the connection between people and their environments and the great shock and damage to well-being that is caused by forced evacuation.

Nevertheless the participants in these films, who bring with them all the ambivalence of human experience, are keen to acknowledge that the industry has been part of an era of prosperity that can also be seen in the architecture and heard in the stories handed down the generations. The lives of thousands of people have been defined by it as can be seen in the films *Under Control* and *Indian Point*. The closure of power stations is mitigated by the process of decommissioning creating a new industry in itself, but the possible lack of continuity marks another kind of loss without renewal that is duly made visible. One of the concerns that came out of the accident at Fukushima concerned the issue of waste stored on the surface, particularly high-level waste held in radioactive fuel pools. This issue, more than any, has prompted greater reflection on the siting of high-level waste repositories in films like *Into Eternity* and *Containment*. Even *Pandora's Promise* and *Return of the Atom* are about the future for an industry in which power production is only one part of a complex of engineering solutions needed to deal with the legacies of the past.

None of the issues addressed in these films is new. What is new are the attempts to find ways to use the camera to express in a more differentiated way the nature of the radioactive substances created and their relationship to the people who work with them. The openness and transparency that was called for in the wake of the accident at Chernobyl and after the accident at Fukushima and which was exemplified first in the documentary films of Shevchenko has been seen as a risk, but it is recognized that it is necessary to bring cultural practices and scientific understanding together into a dynamic reflexive community. Without such a process there is no possibility for the industry to develop in future. The documentaries then are accompanied by a sense that the memories of a generation as they pass into history need to be gathered and reflected on by a new generation in its decision to renew or reject nuclear power.

Atomic: Living in Dread and Promise is, then, the product of an old generation of radioactive documentaries projected at a new one. Cousins labelled it an anti-nuclear showreel designed to be played with the soundtrack very loud. By accident or by design it does more than protest however. By bringing together the archives of government, of the nuclear industry, of nuclear protestors and nuclear promoters, it has created a story that counters attempts to create either a history of achievement or a history of failure. There are many more things that could be discussed in relation to *Atomic*, which reflects a very British response to its nuclear archive – the British Film Institute National Archive is its principal source. Online, Cousins has commented that the film was made very fast (Cousins 2015). Within the film, which is a Creative Scotland production, there is also a specifically Scottish motivation for its structure. A wonderful inclusion is the name of Robert Brown, a Scottish botanist who first observed pollen floating on water in 1827 in a constant state of motion and reorientation and that other small particles, whether alive or not, have a similar motion. Brownian motion only received an explanation in 1905 in a paper by Albert Einstein. For *Atomic* this prompts the inclusion of startlingly clear and beautiful images of moving microscopy and the film goes on to organize its montage as a kind of quasi-Brownian motion, moving around reorganizing an accidental set of archive images from theme to theme, disrupting its chronology by continuously returning to things previously introduced.

To conclude, the process of the cultural assimilation of radioactivity as a phenomenon has been accompanied by documentary photography from the start. There is a very direct relationship between the camera and radioactivity. As media that have played a role in the development of nuclear technology film, analogue video and digital video have been an integral part of the institutional and cultural

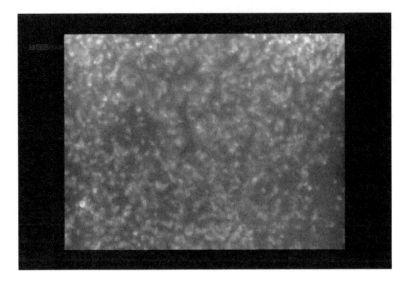

FIGURE 6.2: Brownian motion – the small circles are shown in a state of constant shimmering motion – initiates the cyclical editing of archive material, Mark Cousins (dir.), *Atomic: Living in Dread and Promise*, 2015. United Kingdom. Crossover, Hopscotch Films.

contexts that have formed around the military and civil developments. It is tempting to divide contemporary films and programmes into those that are in some sense an explicit part of the reflexive practical process of public relations and those which reflect on the history of nuclear energy, but the national and international relevance of nuclear issues means there can be no such divide. As long as historical evidence in the form of archive film is presented to explain current issues, it too is part of an ongoing response to current issues.

In the context of the United Kingdom, several BBC programmes are evidence of the continued relevance of television documentary to nuclear history. Not only did *Windscale: Britain's Biggest Nuclear Disaster* (Aspinall 2007) represent the international context for a major accident in 1957, it also considered the government report that was received by the workforce as a cover-up. An episode of BBC television documentary series *Arena*, titled 'A British Guide to the End of the World' (2019), about the H-bomb tests has also demonstrated how the issues pass from generation to generation. Moving outside this institutional context, a new independently made documentary film *The Atom: A Love Affair* (Lesley 2020) takes the exploitation of the archive beyond the national broadcaster, leaving the story completely open in the knowledge that the relationship between the state and nuclear science is continuing as the UK government decides on the funding of future projects. Even the Wilson sisters' experimental documentary, *The Toxic*

Camera (2012) which was part of an installation with the sculpture discussed in the preface, and which offers a reflection on the historicity of documentary as a social discourse, is also engaged with the contemporary experience of living with the uncanny spaces left behind by the Cold War. With a soundtrack rich in associations with nuclear processes, it includes the texts of interviews with the crew who filmed at Chernobyl with Shevchenko. Their stories about the director, delivered by actors in the film, relate how he tried to shield them as they filmed, how he spent hours editing the film, building him into an *auteur* and identifying him with his life as a documentary filmmaker. Made with a high-definition digital camera the Wilsons' film is characteristic for contemporary artists' work with the new medium. They incorporate celluloid film, with its emphasis on the indexical relationship with light, into the digital present through their retro-styled representations of commemorative spaces. The documentary images of a visit to the nuclear waste site, where the camera is buried in lead alongside other equipment that became contaminated in the weeks and months after the accident, are associated through sound overlaps and image editing with a visit to a former military site at Orford Ness in Britain, where testing of nuclear equipment was carried out as part of the British nuclear deterrent.

The Wilsons' and their co-creators' recordings representing Shevchenko's crew, as well as the voices of other veterans of the Chernobyl crisis, reach across different

FIGURE 6.3: Two workers demonstrate the extraction of objects from one of the legacy storage ponds, Tim Usborne (dir.), *Britain's Nuclear Secrets: Inside Sellafield*, 2015. United Kingdom. British Broadcasting Corporation, Artlab Films.

communities affected by nuclear history via the discourses of memory and testimony as well as recordings of architecture and place. By shooting some of their film at a British former atomic weapons testing site at Orford Ness, now preserved by the National Trust, they make the international connection between nuclear sites visible. Creating a composite picture of a history of mutually penetrated secrets showing symmetrical development in different places with similar concrete surfaces, the same kind of contamination requiring the same forms of legacy monitoring and management, they make a gesture about the present that is of a piece with institutional efforts to share past experiences for the sake of the global future. The idea of radioactive documentary has been to continue these thoughts into more of the everyday experience of nuclear sites after the Cold War, such as this frank image of two people using a screen and remotely controlled claws to extract radioactive waste from the murky beginnings of the British atomic project. It is a down-to-earth picture, the domestic outcome to the film *Atoms: A Love Affair*.

This image contributes something different to the communication of nuclear issues. As a representation of an expensive national clean-up operation it poses as many questions about the future of the industry as it answers – anticipating incorporation into a new atomic compilation.

References

Achbar, Mark and Abbott, Jennifer (2003), *The Corporation*, Canada: Big Media Productions.

Alexievich, Svetlana (2016), *Chernobyl Prayer* (trans. A. Gunin and A. Tait), London and New York: Penguin.

Asafu-Adjaye, John, Blomqvist, Linus, Brand, Stewart, Brook, Barry, Defries, Ruth, Ellis, Erle, Foreman, Christopher, Keith, David, Lewis, Martin, Lynas, Mark, Nordhaus, Ted, Pielke Jr, Roger, Pritzker, Rachel, Roy, Joyashree, Sagoff, Mark, Shellenberger, Michael, Stone, Robert and Teague, Peter (2015), 'An ecomodernist manifesto', Eco Modernism, April, http://www.ecomodernism.org/manifesto-english/. Accessed 12 June 2020.

Aspinall, Sarah (2007), *Windscale: Britain's Biggest Nuclear Disaster*, (8 October, UK: BBC)

Assmann, Aleida (2007), *Geschichte im Gedächtnis: Von der individuellen Erfahrung zur öffentlichen Inszenierung*, Munich: C. H. Beck.

'Ästhetik der Atomindustrie' (2011), *Stuttgarter Zeitung*, 11 April, p. 11.

'Atomic Assassin' (2013), C. Bingham (dir.), *River Monsters*, Season 5 Episode 2 (14 April, USA: Animal Planet).

Aubrey, Crispin (ed.) (1982), *Nukespeak: The Media and the Bomb*, London: Comedia Publishing Group.

Aufderheide, Patricia (2016), 'Conversations about impact in documentary: Beyond fear and loathing', *CineAction*, 97, pp. 33–38.

Austrian Film Commission (1999) '*Pripyat* press pack', https://www.geyrhalterfilm.com/pripyat. Accessed 3 October 2020.

Axton, Natalie (2014), 'Film looks between the rock, hard place', The Daily Yonder, 22 October, https://www.dailyyonder.com/film-looks-between-rock-hard-place/2014/10/22/7583/. Accessed 17 June 2020.

Barnouw, Eric (1993), *Documentary: A History of the Non-Fiction Film*, 2nd ed., New York and Oxford: Oxford University Press.

Barthes, Roland (1982), *Camera Lucida: Reflections on Photography*, New York: Hill & Wang.

Beck, John and Bishop, Ryan (eds) (2016), *Cold War Legacies: Systems, Theory, Aesthetics, eBook*, Edinburgh: Edinburgh University Press.

Beck, Ulrich (1992), *Risk Society: Towards a New Modernity* (trans. M. Ritter), London, Thousand Oaks, CA, and New Delhi: Sage.

Beck, Ulrich, Giddens, Anthony and Lash, Scott (1994), *Reflexive Modernization: Politics, Tradition and Aesthetics in the Modern Social Order*, Cambridge, MA: Polity Press.

Beraza, Susan (2013), *Uranium Drive-In: Half Life of the American Dream*, USA: Reel Thing.

Bordwell, David and Thompson, Kristin (1990), *Film Art: An Introduction*, 3rd ed., New York: McGraw Hill.

Bordwell, David, Staiger, Janet and Thompson, Kristin (1988), *The Classical Hollywood Cinema: Film Style and Mode of Production to 1960*, London: Routledge.

Bradshaw, Peter (2010), '*Into Eternity* review', *The Guardian*, 11 November, https://www.theguardian.com/film/2010/nov/11/into-eternity-film-review. Accessed 5 October 2020.

Braun, Peter (2009), 'Von Europa erzählen: Über die Konstruktion der Erinnerung in den Dokumentarfilmen von Volker Koepp', in T. Ebbrecht, H. Hoffmann and J. Schweinitz (eds), *DDR Erinnern Vergessen: Das visuelle Gedächtnis des Dokumentarfilms*, Marburg: Schüren, pp. 71–91.

Bräunig, Werner (2015), *Rummelplatz*, 5th ed., Berlin: Aufbau.

Brionowski, Anna (2004), *Helen's War: Portrait of a Dissident*, Australia: Sonja Armstrong Productions.

British Pathé (1947), *Didcot Atom Village*, UK: British Pathé, https://www.britishpathe.com/video/didcot-atom-village. Accessed 12 June 2020.

'A British Guide to the End of the World' (2019), *Arena* Daniel Vernon (dir.), Season 44, Episode 6 (4 November, UK: BBC).

Carpenter, Ele (2012), 'The culture of nuclear dismantling', *Nuclear Culture*, 20 December, https://nuclear.artscatalyst.org/content/culture-nuclear-dismantling. Accessed 12 June 2020.

Carpenter, Ele (ed.) (2016), *The Nuclear Culture Source Book*, London: Black Dog.

Catsoulis, Jeannette (2011), 'An intimate tour of a gleaming German nuclear plant', *New York Times*, 2 December, p. 10.

Cold War Patriots (2020), Cold War Patriots Website, https://coldwarpatriots.org/. Accessed 12 June 2020.

Connor, Bruce (1976), *Crossroads*, USA: Academy Film Archive.

Courtney, Susan (2018), 'Framing the bomb in the West: The view from lookout mountain', in H. Wasson and L. Grieveson (eds), *Cinema's Military Industrial Complex*, Oakland, CA: University of California Press, pp. 210–26.

Cousins, Mark (2015), *Atomic: Living in Dread and Promise*, UK: Crossover, Hopscotch Films.

Crutzen, Paul. J. and Stoermer, Eugene (2000), 'The Anthropocene', *IGBP Newsletter*, 41:1, pp. 17–18.

Curtiz, Adam (1992), 'A is for Atom', *Pandora's Box*, Episode 6, (16 July, UK: BBC).

de Roulet, Daniel (2011), 'You didn't see anything at Fukushima: Letter to a Japanese friend', in D. de Roulet, A. Waldman, S. Federici, G. Caffentzis and S. Kohso, *Fukushima Mon Amour*, New York: Autonomedia, pp. 7–30.

DeFore, John (2015), 'Return of the Atom' ('Atomin Paluu'), *TIFF Review: The Hollywood Reporter*, 9 October, https://www.hollywoodreporter.com/review/return-atom-atomin-paluu-tiff-820832. Accessed 5 October 2020.

138

Delicath, John W. and DeLuca, Kevin M. (2003), 'Image events, the public sphere, and argumentative practice: The case of radical environmental groups', *Argumentation*, 17:3, pp. 315–33.

DeLuca, Kevin M. (1999), *Image Politics: The New Rhetoric of Environmental Activism*, Kindle ed., New York: The Guildford Press.

Dinitto, Rachel (2014), 'Narrating the cultural trauma of 3/11: The debris of post Fukushima literature and film', *Japan Forum*, 26:3, pp. 340–60.

Dolan, Kerry A. (2013), 'Why billionaire Paul Allen backed pro-nuclear film *Pandora's Promise*', *Forbes*, 14 June, https://www.forbes.com/sites/kerryadolan/2013/06/14/why-billionaire-paul-allen-backed-pro-nuclear-power-film-pandoras-promise/#15ccc9b048a1. Accessed 12 June 2020.

Domenig, Aya (2015), *Als die Sonne vom Himmel fiel* (*The Day the Sun Fell*), Switzerland: ican films, Schweizer Radio und Fernsehen and Finnish Broadcasting Company (YLE).

Dynevor, Gerard (1967), *Nuclear Cathedral*, 21 April, UK: Grenada.

Ebbrecht, Tobias, Hoffmann, Hilde and Schweinitz, Jörg (eds) (2009), *DDR Erinnern, Vergessen: Das visuelle Gedächtnis des Dokumentarfilms*, Marburg: Schüren.

Eisenhower, Dwight D. (2005), 'Farewell radio and television address to the American people', in *Dwight D. Eisenhower: 1960-61: Containing the Public Messages, Speeches, and Statements of the President, January 1, 1960, to January 20, 1961*, Ann Arbor, MI: University of Michigan Library, pp. 1035–40, http://name.umdl.umich.edu/4728424.1960.001. Accessed 12 June 2020.

Eisenhower, Dwight D. (1953), 'Binder 13', *Atoms for Peace*, 8 December, https://www.eisenhower.archives.gov/researches.gov/research/online_documents/atoms_for_peace/Binder13.pdf. Accessed 12 June 2020.

Filmstiftung NRW, Pressestelle (2008), 'Junge Dokumentarfilmer in der Kölner Wolkenburg', *Film und Medienstiftung NRW: Pressearchiv*, 30 July, http://www.filmundmediennrw.de/Archiv/presse_archiv.php?we_objectID=2794. Accessed 17 June 2020.

Flowers, Sir Brian (1976), *Nuclear Power and the Environment: Royal Commission on Environmental Pollution*, London: HMSO, http://www.davidsmythe.org/nuclear/flowers%20commission%201976.pdf. Accessed 12 June 2020.

Foucault, Michel (2002), *The Archaeology of Knowledge*, Abingdon and New York: Routledge.

Foucault, Michel, Manglier, Patrice and Zabunyan, Dork (2018), *Foucault at the Movies* (ed. and trans. C. O'Farrell), New York: Columbia University Press.

Fox, Josh (2010) *Gasland*, USA: International WOW Company.

Fujiwara, Toshi (2011a), 'Interview with Toshi Fujiwara about *No Man's Zone*', *Asian Docs*, 28 December, https://storiadocgiappone.wordpress.com/2015/11/29/interview-with-toshi-fujiwara-about-no-mans-zone-%E7%84%A1%E4%BA%BA%E5%9C%B0%E5%B8%AF-2011/. Accessed 17 June 2020.

Fujiwara, Toshi (2011b), *No Man's Zone*, Japan and France: Aliocha Films, Denis Friedman Productions.

Galison, Peter (1997a), *How Experiments End*, Chicago, IL, and London: University of Chicago Press.

Galison, Peter (1997b), *Image and Logic: Material Culture of Microphysics*, Chicago, IL, and London: University of Chicago Press.

Galison, Peter (2003), *Einstein's Clocks, Poincaré's Maps: Empires of Time*, New York: W. W. Norton

Galison, Peter (2011), 'Waste-wilderness: A conversation with Peter L. Galison', interviewed by J. Kruse, *Friends of the Pleistocene*, 31 March, https://fopnews.wordpress.com/2011/03/31/galison/. Accessed 12 June 2020.

Galison, Peter (2013), 'Socio-technical aspects of nuclear waste and its long term storage', 16 September, *National Science Foundation*, https://www.nsf.gov/awardsearch/showAward?AWD_ID=1256690&HistoricalAwards=false. Accessed 12 June 2020.

Galison, Peter and Moss, Robb (2015), *Containment*, USA and Japan: Redacted Pictures.

Galison, Peter and Moss, Robb (2016), 'Moderated discussion with makers of *Containment* documentary', interviewed by W. Rankin, *Yale University, The Franke Programme in Science and the Humanities*, 25 April, https://frankeprogram.yale.edu/event/screening-containment-discussion-follow. Accessed 12 June 2020.

Galison, Peter and Moss, Robb (2018), *Secrecy*, USA: Redacted Pictures.

Geyrhalter, Nikolaus (1999), *Pripyat*, Austria and Ukraine: Nikolaus Geyrhalter Filmproduction, firstchoicefilms, Österreichischer Rundfunk and Österreichisches Filminstitut.

Glick, Joshua and Musser, Charles (2018), 'Documentary's longue durée: Reimagining the documentary tradition', *World Records*, 2:4, https://vols.worldrecordsjournal.org/02/04. Accessed 12 June 2020.

Goldenberg, Suzanne (2010), 'Barack Obama gives green light to new wave of nuclear reactors', *The Guardian*, 16 February, https://www.theguardian.com/environment/2010/feb/16/barack-obama-nuclear-reactors. Accessed 12 June 2020.

Good, Jennifer L. (2006), 'DVD review *Sun Seekers* by Konrad Wolf', *German Studies Review*, 29:2, pp. 481–82.

Guéret, Eric (2009), *Waste: The Nuclear Nightmare*, France: Bonne Pioch.

Guillaume, Nathalie (2018), 'Hinkley Point C: The biggest construction site in Europe is on track', *Revue Generale Nucleaire*, 1, pp. 54–57.

Gwin, Louis (1990), *Speak No Evil: The Promotional Heritage of Nuclear Risk Communication*, New York: Praeger.

Hamilton, Kevin and O'Gormon, Ned (2019), *Lookout America! The Secret Hollywood Studio at the Heart of the Cold War*, Lebanon: Dartmouth College Press.

Hanich, Julian (2011), 'Bargeldbündel in Beton', *Der Tagesspiegel*, 17 February, p. 30.

Hansen, Miriam (1999), 'Mass production of the senses: Classical cinema as vernacular modernism', *Modernism/Modernity*, 6:2, pp. 59–77.

Heath, Stephen (1975), 'From Brecht to film: Theses, problems', *Screen*, 16:4, pp. 34–45.

Hecht, Heidemarie (1996), 'Der letzte Akt: 1989-1992', in G. Jordan and R. Schenk (eds), *Schwarzweiss und Farbe: DEFA-Dokumentarfilme 1946-1992*, Berlin: Jovis, pp. 234–69.

Hediger, Vincent and Vonderau, Patrick (2009), *Films That Work*, Amsterdam: Amsterdam University Press.

Hefner, Robert A. (2009), *The Grand Energy Transition: The Rise of Energy Gases, Sustainable Life and Growth, and the Next Great Economic Expansion*, Hoboken, New Jersey: John Wiley.

Heller, Chaia (2004), 'Risky science and savoir-faire: Peasant expertise in the French debate over genetically modified crops', in M. E. Lien and B. Nerlich (eds), *The Politics of Food*, Oxford and New York: Berg, pp. 81–99.

Hight, Craig (2013), 'Beyond sobriety: Documentary diversions', in B. Winston (ed.), *The Documentary Film Book*, London: BFI, Palgrave Macmillan, pp. 198–205.

Hilgartner, Stephen, Bell, Richard C. and O'Connor, Rory (1982), *Nukespeak: Nuclear Language, Visions, and Mindset*, San Fransisco: Sierra Club Books.

Hoad, Phil (2016), '*Atomic: Living in Dread and Promise* review: Laborious archival pasteup', *The Guardian*, 20 October, https://www.theguardian.com/film/2016/oct/20/atomic-living-in-dread-and-promise-review. Accessed 17 June 2020.

Hogg, Jonathan (2016), *British Nuclear Culture: Official and Unofficial Narratives in the Long 20th Century*, London and New York: Bloomsbury.

Holden, Stephen (1991), 'Bad times at the A-Bomb factory', *The New York Times*, 12 October, p. 1001020.

Hora, Stephen C. and von Winterfeldt, Detlof (1997), 'Nuclear waste and future societies: A look into the deep future', *Technological Forecasting and Social Change*, 56, pp. 155–70.

Hughes, Helen (2013), 'Arguments without words in *Unser täglich Brot*', *Continuum*, 27:3, pp. 347–64.

Hughes, Helen (2014), *Green Documentary: Environmental Documentary in the Twenty-First Century*, Bristol: Intellect.

Huguet, Benjamin (2016), *The Ray Cat Solution*, USA: Aeon Videos, https://vimeo.com/138843064. Accessed 17 June 2020.

International Atomic Energy Agency (IAEA) (1991), *The International Chernobyl Project*, Vienna: IAEA, https://www.iaea.org/publications/3756/the-international-chernobyl-project. Accessed 17 June 2020.

International Atomic Energy Agency (2004), *Use of Control Room Simulators for Training of Nuclear Power Plant Personnel*, Vienna: IAEA-TECDOC-1411, https://wwwpub.iaea.org/MTCD/publications/PDF/te_1411_web.pdf. Accessed 17 June 2020.

International Nuclear Safety Advisory Group (INSAG) (1993), *The Chernobyl Accident: Updating of INSAG 1*, Vienna: IAEA, https://www.iaea.org/publications/3786/the-chernobyl-accident-updating-of-insag-1. Accessed 17 June 2020.

Jaczko, Greg B. (2019), *Confessions of a Rogue Nuclear Regulator*, New York and London: Simon & Schuster.

Juhasz, Alexandra and Lebow, Alisa (2018), 'Beyond story: An online community-based manifesto', *World Records*, 2:3, https://vols.worldrecordsjournal.org/02/03. Accessed 17 June 2020.

Jungk, Robert (1958), *Brighter than a Thousand Suns: A Personal History of the Atomic Scientists*, New York: Harcourt Brace.

Jungk, Robert (1961), *Children of the Ashes: The People of Hiroshima* (trans. C. Fitzgibbon), London: Pelican.

Jungk, Robert (1979), *The Nuclear State* (trans. E. Mosbacher), London: John Calder.

Jungk, Robert (1990), *Zukunft zwischen Angst und Hoffnung*, 2nd ed., Munich: Wilhelm Heyn.

Jurschick, Karin (2011), *Die Wolke: Tschernobyl und die Folgen* (*The Cloud: Chernobyl and Its Consequences*), Germany: ARTE, Mitteldeutscher Rundfunk and Zero One Film.

Karlsch, Rainer (2011), *Uran für Moskau: Die Wismut: Eine populäre Geschichte*, 4th ed., Berlin: Links.

Khoso, Sabu (2011), 'Fangs hiding in the green: Between revolution and disaster, the world and the earth', in D. de Roulet, A. Waldman, S. Federici, G. Caffentzis and S. Kohso, *Fukushima Mon Amour*, New York: Autonomedia, pp. 47–68.

Kinsella, William J. (2005), 'One hundred years of nuclear discourse: Four master themes and their implications for environmental communication', in N. J. Mahway, *The Environmental Communication Yearbook*, London: Lawrence Erlbaum, pp. 49–72.

Kivenen, Kati (2013), 'Perceptible radiation: Creative documentarism and experientialist essayism in Mika Taanila's video installation *The Most Electrified Town in Finland*', in M. Taanila, *Aikakoneita* (*Time Machines*), exhibition catalogue, Museum of Contemporary Art Kiasma, Helsinki, 1 November 2013–2 March 2014, pp. 75–82.

Knight, Derrick (prod.) (1959), *March to Aldermaston*, UK: Film and Television Committee for Nuclear Disarmament.

Koehler, Robert (2011), 'Review of *Under Control*', *Daily Variety*, 29 April, https://variety.com/2011/scene/reviews/under-control-1117945117/. Accessed 17 June 2020.

Koepp, Volker (1991), *Wismut*, Germany: Südwestfunk, Westdeutscher Rundfunk, ö-film.

Koepp, Volker (1995a), *Kalte Heimat* (*Cold Homeland*), Germany: Dokumentarfilm Babelsberg.

Koepp, Volker (1995b), 'Meine Arbeit bei der DEFA', in P. Zimmermann (ed.), *Deutschlandbilder Ost: Dokumentarfilme der DEFA von der Nachkriegszeit bis zur Wiedervereinigung*, Konstanz: Ölschläger, pp. 151–54.

Koepp, Volker and Nowak, Andreas (1995), 'Neues in Wittstock: Neues vom Dokumentarfilm: Ein Gespräch mit dem Regisseur Volker Koepp', in P. Zimmermann (ed.), *Deutschlandbilder Ost: Dokumentarfilme der DEFA von der Nachkriegszeit bix zur Wiedervereinigung*, Konstanz: Ölschläger, pp. 155–59.

Konner, Joan (1977), *Danger! Radioactive Waste*, USA: NBC.

Kriest, Ulrich (2011), 'Männer, die auf Lämpchen starren', *Stuttgarter Zeitung*, 26 May, p. 29.

Krukones, James H. (1991), 'The Glasnost Film Festival (review)', *American Historical Review*, pp. 1134–38.

Kyander, Pontus (2013), 'Licking frogs in the dark: Mika Taanila's *Science Noir* trilogy', in M. Taanila, *Aikakoneita* (*Time Machines*), exhibition catalogue, Museum of Contemporary Art Kiasma, Helsinki, 1 November 2013–2 March 2014, p. 908.

Latour, Bruno (2004), *Politics of Nature: How to Bring the Sciences into Democracy* (trans. C. Porter), Cambridge, MA, and London: Harvard University Press.

Laucht, Christoph (2012), 'Atoms for the people: The Atomic Scientists Association, the British state and nuclear education in the *Atom Train* exhibition, 1947–1948', *British Journal for the History of Science*, 45:4, pp. 591–608.

Leser, Julia and Seidel, Claudia (2011), *Radioactivists: Protest in Japan since Fukushima*, Germany: Ginger & Blonde Productions.

Lesley, Vicki (2020), *The Atom: A Love Affair*, UK: Tenner Films, Dartmouth Films.

Lim, Dennis (2011), 'Catastrophe filmmaking in Japan', 16 March, *International Herald Tribune*, p. 15.

Lippit, Akira M. (2005), *Atomic Light (Shadow Optics)*, Minneapolis and London: University of Minnesota Press.

Lowry, David (2015), '*Inside Sellafield* and military plutonium: The BBC's nuclear lies of omission', *Ecologist*, 12 August, https://theecologist.org/2015/aug/12/inside-sellafield-and-military-plutonium-bbcs-nuclear-lies-omission. Accessed 17 June 2020.

Lüthge, Katja (2011), 'Kathedralen der Kernspaltung: Schönheit und Schrecken', *Frankfurter Rundschau*, 26 May, p. 30.

Madsen, Michael (2008), *Into Eternity: A Film for the Future*, Denmark, Finland, Sweden and Italy: Atmo Media Network, Film I Väst, Global HDTV, Magic Hour Films, Mouka Filmi Oi and Yleisradio.

Madsen, Michael (2011), 'Conversation with Michael Madsen: Director of *Into Eternity*', Friends of the Pleistocene, 31 January, https://fopnews.wordpress.com/2011/01/31/conversation-with-michael-madsen-director-of-into-eternity/. Accessed 17 June 2020.

Marder, Michael and Tondeur, Anaïs (2016), *The Chernobyl Herbarium: Fragments of an Exploded Consciousness*, London: Open Humanities Press.

Mauersberger, Kerstin and Ast, Jürgen (2011), *Wildwest bei der Wismut: Atombomben aus dem Erzgebirge*, Germany: Astfilm Productions and Mitteldeutscher Rundfunk.

McNeill, David and Matsumoto, Chie (2017), 'In Fukushima, a land where few return', *Japan Times*, 13 May, https://www.japantimes.co.jp/news/2017/05/13/national/socialissues/fukushima-land-return/#.W_V_Guj7TvY. Accessed 17 June 2020.

McNeill, John Robert and Engelke, Peter (2014), *The Great Acceleration: An Environmental History of the Anthropocene since 1945*, Cambridge, MA: Harvard University Press.

Meeropol, Ivy (2015), *Indian Point*, Japan, USA: Motto Pictures, Red 50.

Meeropol, Ivy (2016), 'Q&A: Ivy Meeropol', Film Society Lincoln Centre, 8 July, https://www.youtube.com/watch?v=hs9Ria-5zkU. Accessed 17 June 2020.

Mellott, Greg (2012), *The Grand Energy Transition*, USA: Gray Hour.

Meyer, Jan Henrik, (2017) 'An overview of the historical experience of nuclear energy and society in 20 countries', draft brochure, *History of Nuclear Energy and Society Consortium* (HoNESt), Deliverable No 3.6, http://honest2020.eu/sites/all/themes/Porto_sub/downloads/Summary_short_country_reports.pdf. Accessed 16 November 2020.

Messmer, Susanne (2011), 'Kurz und Kritisch', 11 February, *Tageszeitung*, p. 30.

Michelsen, Karl-Erik and Harjula, Aisulu (2017), 'Finland Short Country Report (version 2017)' in *History of Nuclear Energy and Society* Consortium (HoNESt), deliverable No. 3.6, http://www.honest2020.eu/sites/default/files/deliverables_24/FI.pdf. Accessed 5 October 2020.

Minh-ha, Trinh T. (1993), 'The totalizing quest of meaning', in M. Renov, *Theorizing Documentary*, New York and London: Routledge, pp. 90–107.

Moore, J. P. (2013), 'J. P. Moore's interview', interviewed by J. Elmingler, The Voices of the Manhattan Project, 28 June, https://www.manhattanprojectvoices.org/oral-histories/j-p-moores-interview. Accessed 17 June 2020.

Mori, Mark and Robinson, Susan (1991), *Building Bombs*, USA: Single Spark Pictures.

Morton, Timothy (2013), *Hyperobjects: Philosophy and Ecology after the End of the World*, Minneapolis: University of Minnesota Press.

Nakahara, Shinji and Ichikawa, Masao (2013), 'Mortality in the 2011 tsunami in Japan', *Journal of Epidemiology*, 23:1, pp. 70–73.

Nichols, Bill (1983), 'The voice of documentary', *Film Quarterly*, 36:3, pp. 17–30.

Nichols, Bill(1991), *Representing Reality: Issues and Concepts in Documentary*, Bloomington, IN: Indiana University Press.

Nichols, Bill (1994), *Blurred Boundaries and Questions of Meaning in Contemporary Culture*, Bloomington, IN: Indiana University Press.

Nichols, Bill (2017), *Introduction to Documentary*, 3rd ed., Bloomington, IN: Indiana University Press.

Nikolaus Geyrhalter Filmproduktion (1999), 'Pripyat press material', Geyrhalterfilm, https://www.geyrhalterfilm.com/en/pripyat. Accessed 12 June 2020.

Nixon, Rob (2013), *Slow Violence, Gender, and the Environmentalism of the Poor*, Cambridge, MA: Harvard University Press.

OECD Nuclear Energy Agency (1995), 'Chernobyl ten years on', OECD Nuclear Energy Agency, https://www.oecd-nea.org/rp/chernobyl/chernobyl-1995.pdf. Accessed 5 October 2020.

OECD Nuclear Energy Agency (2002), 'Chernobyl: Assessment of radiological and health impacts – 2002 update of Chernobyl ten years on', The NEA Nuclear Energy Agency, https://www.oecd-nea.org/rp/pubs/2003/3508-chernobyl.pdf. Accessed 5 October 2020.

Office of Civil Defense (1951), *Duck and Cover*, USA: Archer Productions.

'Our Friend the Atom' (1957), Hamilton S. Luske (dir.), *Walt Disney's Wonderful World of Color* (23 January, NBC, USA: Walt Disney Productions).

Plokhy, Serhii (2018), *Chernobyl: History of a Tragedy*, London: Penguin, Allen Lane.

Rafael, Joana (2009), 'Architecture on film: *Pripyat*', Architecture Foundation, 12 May, http://www.architecturefoundation.org.uk/programme/2009/architecture-on-film/pripyat. Accessed 5 October 2020.

Rafferty, Kevin, Loader, Jayne and Rafferty, Pierce (1982), *The Atomic Café*, USA: The Archives Project.

Reel Thing (2013), 'UDI press kit', Uranium Drive-In, 15 January, http://uraniumdrivein.com/img/press/UDI_press_kit_01.15.14_compressed.pdf. Accessed 17 June 2020.

Reeve, John (1956), *Atomic Achievement*, UK: Rayant Productions.

Renck, Johan (2019), *Chernobyl*, USA: HBO.

Renov, Michael (ed.) (1993a), *Theorizing Documentary*, New York and London: Routledge.

Renov, Michael (1993b), 'Toward a poetics of documentary', in M. Renov (ed.), *Theorizing Documentary*, New York and London: Routledge, pp. 12–36.

Reuters (1987), 'A Soviet filmmaker at Chernobyl in '86 is dead of radiation', *New York Times*, 30 May, p. 1001005, https://www.nytimes.com/1987/05/30/world/a-soviet-film-maker-at-chernobyl-in-86-is-dead-of-radiation.html. Accessed 17 June 2020.

Roberts, Graham (2000), *The Man with the Movie Camera: The Film Companion*, London: I. B. Tauris.

Robinson, Susan J. (2007), 'Filmmaker interviews', *Building Bombs*, DVD extras, USA: Docuramafilms.

Romer, Alfred (1970), *Radiochemistry and the Discovery of Isotopes*, New York: Dover Publications.

Ronder, Paul (1969), *Hiroshima–Nagasaki August 1945*, USA: Museum of Modern Art Film Library, https://archive.org/details/hiroshimanagasakiaugust1945. Accessed 5 October 2020.

Royal College of Art (2018), 'The toxic camera', *Archive of Research Processes and Output Produced by RCA*, 9 November, http://researchonline.rca.ac.uk/1744/. Accessed 17 June 2020.

Sarkar, Bhaskar and Walker, Janet (2010), *Documentary Testimonies: Global Archives of Suffering*, New York and London: Routledge.

Sattel, Volker (2011a), 'Eine Welt der Boys and Toys', interviewed by S. Messmer, *taz Berliner Tageszeitung*, 6 April, n.pag.

Sattel, Volker (2011b), 'Inside the atomic industry', interviewed by C. Schaer, *Der Spiegel*, 17 February, http://www.spiegel.de/international/zeitgeist/inside-the-atomic-industry-in-germany-nuclear-power-has-been-demonized-a-746099.html. Accessed 17 June 2020.

Sattel, Volker (2011c), *Unter Kontrolle* (*Under Control*), Germany: Credofilm, Westdeutscher Rundfunk, ARTE.

Schaer, Cathrin (2011) 'Behind the screens: The best actors are smart – and short', *The New Zealand Herald*, 13 February, https://www.nzherald.co.nz/entertainment/news/article.cfm?c_id=1501119&objectid=10705979. Accessed 5 October 2020.

Schieber, Elke (1996), 'Im Dämmerlicht der Perestroike: 1980 bis 1989', in G. Jordan and R. Schenk (eds), *Schwarzweiss und Farbe: DEFA-Dokumentarfilme 1946–92*, Berlin: Jovis, pp. 180–233.

Schreiber, Eduard (1996), 'Zeit der verpassten Möglichkeiten: 1970 bis 1980', in G. Jordan and R. Schenk (eds), *Schwarzweiss und Farbe: DEFA-Dokumentarfilme 1946–92*, Berlin: Jovis, pp. 128–79.

Schulz-Ojala, Jan (2011), 'Wir wissen nichts, aber Bescheid', *Der Tagesspiegel*, 16 March, p. 30.

Schuppli, Susan (2010), 'The most dangerous film in the world', in F. Le Roy, N. Wynants and D. H. Vanderbeeken (eds), *Tickle Your Catastrophe*, Ghent: Ghent University, the KASK (Ghent Royal Academy of Fine Arts) and Vooruit, pp. 130–45.

Schütte, Uwe (2020), *Kraftwerk: Future Music from Germany*, London: Penguin.

Schütterle, Juliane (2010), *Kumpel, Kader und Genossen: Arbeiten und Leben im Uranbergbau der DDR*, Paderborn: Ferdinand Schöningh.

Searle, Adrian (2012), 'Post-atrocity exhibition: Jane and Louise Wilson's disturbing films', *The Guardian*, 22 October, https://www.theguardian.com/artanddesign/2012/oct/22/jane-and-louise-wilson-exhibition. Accessed 17 June 2020.

Sebeok, Thomas A. (1984), *Communication Measures to Bridge Ten Millenia*, Springfield: Research Centre for Language and Semiotic Studies, Indiana University, for Office of Nuclear Waste Isolation and the Batelle Memorial Institute.

Sergienko, Rollan (1987), *Kolokol Chernobyl (The Toxin of Chernobyl)*, USSR: Moscow Central Studio for Documentary Films.

Shapiro, Jerome F. (2001), *Atomic Bomb Cinema*, New York and London: Routledge.

Shevchenko, Vladimir (1987), *Chernobyl: Khronika trudnykh nedel (Chernobyl: A Chronicle of Difficult Weeks)*, Soviet Union: Ukrainian Newsreel and Documentary Film Studio.

Stone, Robert (2009), *The Documentary: Politics, Emotion, Culture*, Basingstoke and New York: Palgrave Macmillan.

Stone, Robert (2016), *Regarding Life: Animals and the Documentary Moving Image*, New York: SUNY.

Stone, Robert (1987), *Radio Bikini*, USA: Crossroads, Robert Stone Productions and WGBH.

Stone, Robert (2013a), *Pandora's Promise*, USA: Robert Stone Productions and Vulcan Productions.

Stone, Robert (2013b), '*Pandora's Promise* director defends his controversial nuclear energy film', Edition CNN, 8 November, https://edition.cnn.com/2013/11/07/opinion/pandora-nuclear-stone-ifr-response/index.html. Accessed 17 June 2020.

Taanila, Mika (2013), *Aikakoneita (Time Machines)*, exhibition catalogue, Museum of Contemporary Art Kiasma, Helsinki, 1 November 2013–2 March 2014.

Taanila, Mika and Eerola, Jussi (2015), *Atomin Paluu (Return of the Atom)*, Finland: Kinotar, Blinker Filmproduktion, Westdeutscher Rundfunk, Yleisradio and ZDF/ARTE.

Taylor, Simon (2016), *The Fall and Rise of Nuclear Power in Britain: A History*, Kindle ed., Cambridge: UIT Cambridge.

Thanouli, Eleftheria (2019), *History and Film: A Tale of Two Disciplines*, New York and London: Bloomsbury.

Thatcher, Margaret (1989), 'Speech to United Nations General Assembly (global environment)', Margaret Thatcher Foundation, https://www.margaretthatcher.org/document/107817. Accessed 5 October 2020.

The Chernobyl Forum (2006), 'Chernobyl's legacy: Health, environmental and socio-economic impacts', IAEA International Atomic Energy Agency, https://www.iaea.org/sites/default/files/chernobyl.pdf. Accessed 5 October 2020.

The Durango Herald (2013), 'Telluride director takes a hard look at uranium', *The Denver Post*, 28 November, https://www.denverpost.com/2013/11/28/telluride-director-takes-a-hard-look-at-uranium/. Accessed 17 June 2020.

The National Diet of Japan Fukushima Nuclear Accident Independent Investigation Commission (2012), 'The official report of the Fukushima Nuclear Accident Independent Investigation Committee executive summary', *NIRS*, https://www.nirs.org/wpcontent/uploads/fukushima/naiic_report.pdf. Accessed 17 June 2020.

The Proper People (2019), 'Exploring an abandoned power plant', *The Proper People*, 28 September, https://www.youtube.com/watch?v=ONEm1ph3MP4. Accessed 17 June 2020.

The World Nuclear Association (2020), 'Radioactive waste management', *World Nuclear*, http://www.world-nuclear.org/information-library/nuclear-fuel-cycle/nuclear-wastes/radio-active-waste-management.aspx. Accessed 17 June 2020.

Thein, Ulrich (1966), *Columbus 64*, German Democratic Republic: Deutscher Fernsehfunk.

Trauth, Kathleen M., Hora, Stephen C. and Guzowski, Robert V. (1993), 'Expert judgement on markers to deter inadvertant human intrusion into the Waste Isolation Pilot Plant', Alberquerque, NM, and Livermore, CA: Sandia National Laboratories for the United States Department of Energy.

Tschirner, Joachim and Drachsel, Burghard (2007), *Die Wismut: terra incognita*, Germany: Um Welt Film.

Tschirner, Joachim and Drachsel, Burghard (2016), *Die Wismut: terra incognita No. 2*, Germany: Um Welt Film.

Turcanu, Catrinel, Schröder, Jantine, Meskens, Gaston, Perko, Tanja, Rossignol, Nicolas, Carlé, Benny and Hardeman, Frank (2015), 'Like a bridge over troubled water: Opening pathways for integrating social sciences and humanities into nuclear research', *Journal of Environmental Radioactivity*, 153, pp. 88–96.

Union Carbide Corporation (1956), *The Petrified River: The Story of Uranium*, New York: Union Carbide and Carbon Corporation.

United Kingdom Warning and Monitoring Organisation (UKWMO) (1971), *Sound an Alarm*, London: UKWMO.

United States Environmental Protection Agency (EPA) (2018), 'Uravan Uranium Project', *Superfund*, 23 October, https://cumulis.epa.gov/supercpad/cursites/csitinfo.cfm?id=0800076. Accessed 17 June 2020.

United States v. Reynolds, 345 (U.S. Supreme Court March 9, 1953), https://supreme.justia.com/cases/federal/us/345/1/. Accessed 17 June 2020.

Uranium Film Festival (2020), 'International Uranium Film Festival: The Atomic Age Film Festival', http://uraniumfilmfestival.org/. Accessed 17 June 2020.

Urbano, Carl (1952), *A is for Atom*, USA: John Sutherland Productions.

Usborne, Tim (2015), *Britain's Nuclear Secrets: Inside Sellafield*, UK: British Broadcasting Corporation and Artlab Films.

Usborne, Tim (2020), 'How we split the atom for a television programme', BBC, https://www.bbc.co.uk/programmes/articles/1fJQlwy1KY775HflGHFvxWK/how-we-split-the-atom-for-a-television-programme. Accessed 17 June 2020.

Walker, Janet (2010), 'Rights and return: Perils and phantasies of situated testimony after Katrina', in B. Sarkar and J. Walker (eds), *Documentary Testimonies: Global Archives of Suffering*, New York and London: Routledge, pp. 83–114.

Wagner, Paul Werner (2012), *DVD Booklet, Der Fernsehfilm 'Columbus 64'*, Hamburg: Studio Hamburg Enterprises.

Wasson, Haidee and Grieveson, Lee (eds) (2018), *Cinema's Military Industrial Complex*, Oakland, CA: University of California Press.

Watkins, Peter (1965), *The War Game*, UK: BBC.

Weart, Spencer R. (1988), *Nuclear Fear: A History of Images*, Cambridge, MA and London: Harvard University Press.

W-Film Distribution (2013), 'About the film chronology', *Journey*, https://diereisezumsicherstenortdererde.ch/en/about-the-film/chronology.html. Accessed 17 June 2020.

Wilson, Jane and Wilson, Louise (2012), *The Toxic Camera*, UK: Wilson Sisters.

Wilson, Jane and Wilson, Louise (2016), '*RCA Fine Art Talk: Jane and Louise Wilson*', Royal College of Art, 20 April, https://vimeo.com/165315554. Accessed 17 June 2020.

Winston, Brian (1995), *Claiming the Real: The Documentary Film Revisited*, London: BFI.

Winston, Brian (2008), *Claiming the Real II: Documentary: Grierson and Beyond*, 2nd ed., London: BFI and Palgrave Macmillan.

Wolf, Konrad (1958), *Sonnensucher* (*Sun Seekers*), GDR: DEFA.

World Nuclear Association (2019), 'Chernobyl Accident 1986', World Nuclear Association, https://www.world-nuclear.org/information-library/safety-and-security/safety-of-plants/chernobyl-accident.aspx. Accessed 17 June 2020.

Young, Neil (2012), 'Toshi Fujiwara's doc chronicles the aftermath of last year's earthquake, tsunami and nuclear disaster in Japan', *Hollywood Reporter*, 29 February, https://www.hollywoodreporter.com/review/no-mans-zone-berlin-film-295984. Accessed 17 June 2020.

Zabolotnyi, Serhiy (2011), *Chernobyl 3828*, Ukraine: Telecon Studio.

Zabunyan, Dork (2018), 'What film is able to do: Foucault and cinematic knowledge', in M. Foucault et al., *Foucault at the Movies*, New York: Columbia University Press, pp. 3–34.

Index

Page numbers in italics refer to figures.